bitcoin
PROFIT SECRETS

The Complete Guide To Mastering And Profiting From Bitcoin

Table Of Contents

Introduction - What Is Bitcoin and Cryptocurrency?

In this guide, you will learn all about Bitcoin (BTC) and cryptocurrency, how they work, why they exist and what kind of technology is behind Bitcoin. It wasn't too long ago when people started hearing the words 'Bitcoin' and 'cryptocurrencies.'

Few people outside of the crypto-communities knew what they were and many thought it was just another fad that was bound to fail in a few years or so. The value of one bitcoin was just a few cents then so obviously it wasn't worth a lot. For this reason, it was ignored by the masses. There were far more profitable investments one could make, after all.

Those who invested sums of money on the new digital currency either believed in the system proposed by its founder, Satoshi Nakamoto, or they simply wanted to see how it works.

> *Either way, those who believed were rewarded greatly, and continue to be rewarded, as a single bitcoin now costs thousands of dollars.*

It only took Bitcoin five years to breach the $1,000 mark in late 2013, and just a few years later, Bitcoin prices are at an all-time high – way past the $10,000 mark for a single bitcoin!

With skyrocketing prices and extremely fast growth, more and more people are curious about bitcoins and cryptocurrencies as a whole.

Cryptocurrencies are digital currencies which are electronic in nature. They do not have a physical form like paper money or coins which you probably have in your wallet right now. You can't hold them physically, but you can buy things with them.

Depending on the merchant you're doing business with, they may accept more than one cryptocurrency as payment.

According to CoinMarketCap (https://coinmarketcap.com), there are more than 1,000 active cryptocurrencies right now. If you're looking to invest your hard-earned cash but can't afford Bitcoin prices right now, there are plenty of alternative cryptocurrencies to choose from such as Ethereum, Litecoin, Ripple, Dash, Monero, Zcash, and more.

We would, of course, advise you to do some in-depth research on the cryptocurrency you want to invest in as not all cryptocurrencies are equal. Some are more stable than others and would, therefore, make for better investments.

Bitcoin is not the world's first cryptocurrency, but it is the most successful. Many have come before it but all have failed. And the reason for failure? Virtual currency had an inherent problem — it was easy to double spend.

You could pay $100 to one merchant and use the same amount of money to pay a second merchant! Scammers and fraudsters simply loved this loophole.

Fortunately, in 2007, Satoshi Nakamoto started working on the Bitcoin concept. On October 31st the following year, he released his white paper entitled "*Bitcoin: A Peer-to-Peer Electronic Cash System*" which outlined a payment system that addressed the double spending problem of digital currencies.

It was a brilliant concept that drew the attention of the cryptographic community. The Bitcoin Project software was registered in SourceForge just a little over a week after the white paper was published.

In January 2009, the first ever Bitcoin block called the 'Genesis block' was mined. Days later, block 170 recorded the first ever bitcoin transaction between Hal Finney and Satoshi Nakamoto.

The very next year, in November 2010, Bitcoin's market cap exceeded $1,000,000! This was a very pivotal moment in the development of Bitcoin as this lead to more people getting interested and investing in bitcoins. The price at this point was $0.50/BTC.

However, in June 2011, Bitcoin experienced the so-called "Great Bubble of 2011" after reaching an all-time high of $31.91/BTC. Just 4 days after reaching its highest price, the exchange rate plummeted to just $10/BTC.

Many investors panicked at losing so much money and sold at a loss. It took almost 2 years for the exchange rate to recover and surpass the previous all-time high. Those who kept their bitcoins made the right decision as the price has continued to climb and surpass everyone's expectations.

What's really interesting about Bitcoin is that while all transactions are public and nothing is hidden from anyone, no one actually knows anything about Satoshi Nakamoto.

Many have speculated that he is not just one person but rather a collective pseudonym for a group of cryptographic developers. Some have come forward claiming to be Satoshi, but to date, his real identity remains a secret.

Why Do Cryptocurrencies Exist?

Many people have started thinking that cryptocurrencies, Bitcoin in particular, are on the brink of replacing our national currencies such as the US Dollar, British Pound Sterling, Euro, Canadian Dollars, and more. This is because cryptocurrencies have started to become very viable alternatives to traditional currency.

Cryptocurrencies exist to address weaknesses in traditional currencies which are, of course, backed by central banks and governments. This makes traditional currencies prone to corruption and manipulation, among a host of other issues.

> *Unlike traditional currencies, there is no governing body that backs Bitcoin and other cryptocurrencies which means they aren't subjected to anybody's whims.*

Bitcoin is completely decentralized, open source and transparent. This means that you can see all the transactions that have ever been done on the network and you can check and review the blockchain data yourself to verify the authenticity of each transaction.

Bitcoin runs on highly complex mathematical algorithms to regulate the creation of new bitcoins and to make sure no double spending ever occurs on the network (remember, this is the Achilles' heel of failed virtual currencies before Bitcoin).

The Bitcoin code is so secure and advanced that it's virtually impossible to cheat the system so if you're thinking you can create an unlimited number of bitcoins, you're greatly mistaken.

One of the main problems of traditional currency is that these aren't limited in number. This means that governments and central banks can print more money when they see fit.

When more money is printed and enters the economy, this reduces the purchasing power of our paper money which means we need to spend more for an item we've only spent a few dollars on before; this is called inflation.

Bitcoin, on the other hand, is a different story. The Bitcoin Protocol states that only 21,000,000 bitcoins can ever be mined and created which means that bitcoin is, in fact, a scarce resource.

Also, like national currencies, bitcoins are divisible, much like cents to a dollar. The smallest bitcoin unit is called a Satoshi, and it is 1/100,000,000 of a bitcoin. This means you can invest a few thousand Satoshis at a time until you finally get a whole bitcoin.

Of course, if you go this route, it may take you some time to get to 1 BTC but if the price continues to skyrocket, then buying a few Satoshis regularly may pay off in the long term.

Another reason why cryptocurrencies are gaining in popularity is that it is highly portable which means you can bring it with you anywhere you go. You can do the same with physical money and gold. However, a large amount will lead to a heavy load on your wallet or bag.

Try putting a million dollars in a briefcase or carrying a bag of gold! It's certainly not as light as it looks in movies.

> *With cryptocurrency, you have different wallet choices, all of which are highly portable, so you can easily make payments whenever and wherever you want.*

Bitcoins are not subject to bank and government regulations. This means you don't need to pay those hefty bank fees which you incur whenever you send payments to other people.

You also don't need to wait several hours or maybe even a few days for your payments to clear or post as bitcoin payments are made almost instantly (usually in 10-45 minutes).

How Bitcoin Works

In this section, we will do our best to explain the Bitcoin process as simply as possible without going into too much technical jargon.

The first thing you need to do is get yourself some bitcoins. You can either mine this yourself, receive some as payment for goods or services, or buy at a Bitcoin exchange like Coinbase or Kraken. There are different wallets for you to store your new bitcoins in.

You can use a desktop wallet, mobile app wallet, paper wallet, hardware wallet or an online wallet. There are pros and cons to each type of wallet.

However, most experts agree that online wallets, specifically those on exchange sites, are not so secure because both your private and public keys are saved online. This makes your wallet highly vulnerable to hackers.

When you've selected the most suitable wallet for your needs, you can then start making bitcoin transactions. To send bitcoin to another user, all you have to do is just get their email or bitcoin address, enter the amount you wish to send, write a quick note to tell them what the payment is for (this is optional), and hit the Send button!

Alternatively, if you've got the QR code to their bitcoin wallet, you can simply scan it and hit Send. The transaction will appear in the other person's account in a short period of time, usually between 10-45 minutes. The reason for this 'wait' is explained more fully in the next section.

And that's it! Bitcoin transactions are quick, safe, cheap and the perfect alternative to paying with bank-issued credit and debit cards, and even paying in cash.

The Technology Behind Bitcoin

On the surface, Bitcoin transactions appear to be fast and easy – and they truly are. However, behind the scenes, the technology that makes the Bitcoin network run seamlessly is a massive ledger known as the blockchain.

It's massive because it contains a record of all bitcoin transactions that have ever taken place since Bitcoin was first released in 2009.

As more time passes by and more transactions occur, the size of the blockchain will continue to grow.   So here is how the blockchain works:

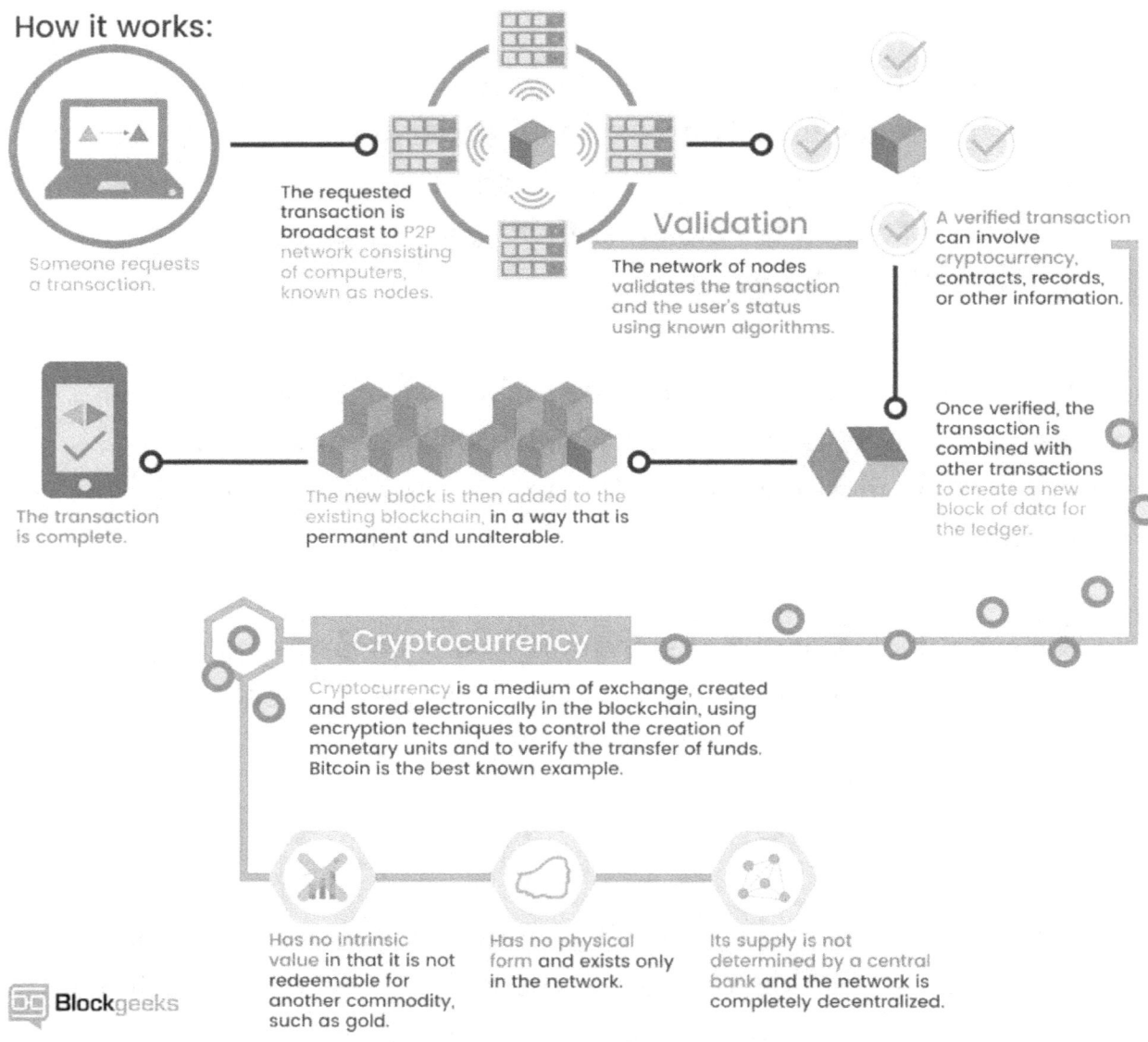

(Image Source: BlockGeeks.com)

When you send a payment, your wallet or app sends out a request to the entire Bitcoin network which is made up of computers or nodes. These nodes then validate your transaction using known algorithms.

Once your transaction is verified and confirmed, it is then combined with other transactions to create a new block of data for the blockchain.

This new block is then added to the end of the blockchain. When this happens, the transaction becomes complete and is now permanent.

This entire process takes about 10-45 minutes from start to finish (this is why Bitcoin transactions don't happen instantly). Once the transaction is finalized, no one can undo or delete the transaction. The person you've sent the bitcoin payment to (the receiver) will now see your payment in his wallet.

So who verifies and confirms transactions if there's no central body governing the network?

The answer is the miners. The miners are literally the lifeblood of the entire bitcoin network. Some have even compared miners to being hamsters in the wheel that keep the entire Bitcoin network going! And this is true.

Miners play such a huge role in the success of Bitcoin that they truly deserve getting rewarded in precious bitcoins. Without them, no new blocks would be created and added to the blockchain.

If nothing is added to the blockchain, no transactions are ever finalized. This means no bitcoins payments are sent and received by anyone on the network. No new bitcoins will be created.

Because miners are indispensable to the Bitcoin network, they are compensated for their hard work in terms of bitcoins (it would not make any sense to reward them in traditional paper currency). They are almost like employees of the network.

Since there are only a limited number of bitcoins (21 million), the number of bitcoins that miners are paid with will continue to dwindle until all bitcoins are exhausted by around 2140.

Now that you know what Bitcoin and cryptocurrency are all about, let's go to the next guide where you will learn how the value of bitcoin is determined.

Bitcoin Value – How Is The Value Of Bitcoin Determined

Bitcoin has been getting a huge amount of hype recently. It's one of the many digital currencies in existence today which acts and functions like regular money but exists entirely electronically—like data inside computers.

And that can be kind of confusing, because if there is no actual physical bitcoin:

- How can it have value?
- How can you use digital currency in a physical world?

Well actually, the question of how bitcoin has any value at all isn't so far off from the question of how most real-world money has value.

First off, Bitcoin has no actual intrinsic value, which means that it has little to no use to us outside of its economic context. But the same can be said for most real-world currencies: money only has value because the government that issues it says it does.

> *This is called 'fiat currency,' because its value is not tied to any physical commodity and relies on the backing of a government.*

But unlike fiat currency, Bitcoin does not have an issuing authority that gives it value. Bitcoin is a decentralized currency, meaning there is no governing body that regulates its production and transactions.

It doesn't answer to any government or organization, so there isn't really a reason why it should have value, yet it does - and it can all be boiled down to utility, scarcity, and supply and demand.

Bitcoin's Value Lies In Its Utility

Before we discuss the utility of Bitcoin, first you must understand the basics of how it works. You are connected to the community of Bitcoin users through a computer network, and the ledgers that Bitcoin uses is called a blockchain: transactions are compiled into blocks, which in turn are connected in a chain-like manner, hence the name.

The ledger keepers are called miners, because what they are doing, essentially, sounds very much like gold miners who work hard to find gold: they are working for the reward in the form of bitcoins, which, like gold, are limited in supply.

So now you know how Bitcoin works. What does that have to do with its value? Everything, actually. Bitcoin's value is in its utility: its decentralization, security, and ease of transaction.

First, let's look at Bitcoin's decentralized system. Bitcoin is designed such that there is no need for any governing authority to control it. It operates through a peer-to-peer network where all transactions are recorded in the blockchain.

On the most basic level, this would mean that it is not tied to any state and therefore is the only truly borderless currency. What this means is that you can conduct transactions with people from different countries easily because you're using the same currency.

On a deeper, much more complicated level, the decentralization of Bitcoin's system creates the possibility of transforming the finance industry.

The finance industry offers multiple ways to simplify transactions for ease of convenience. There are credit and debit cards, money transferring systems, electronic bank transfers, etc. But all of these systems need to have a middleman to function—they need a company or authority to facilitate the exchange.

And what you're doing whenever you make a transaction is that you're putting your trust on the middleman—that they will get your money through or keep your money safe among other things. There is also the matter of transaction fees, which, considered per transaction, is not too much, but can easily pile up over time. What Bitcoin does is it eliminates the need for these middlemen.

As mentioned above, all transactions in the Bitcoin network are recorded in the blockchain by miners. While the blockchain and miner network has the semblance of a governing body in the sense that it keeps track of all bitcoins in existence, it's still in the public domain and therefore cannot be monopolized.

> *This means that no single person or group of persons has a hold on the network—which, in turn, means that bitcoins can remain fully transparent and neutral in its transactions.*

But if there is no official body acting as a regulator, who can you trust to make sure that transactions do go through? The answer: no one. And it sounds bad, but it's actually a good thing.

The Bitcoin system is designed to operate without the need for trust. See, it's not simply a digital currency, it's a *crypto*currency, which means that it is heavily based on encryption techniques to keep it safe.

Instead of operating based on customer trust, Bitcoin operates using tried and tested mathematics (more on that later). Cheating the network is impossible due to its public environment.

Not only that, but the system is encrypted so that trying to commit fraud would require an *extremely large* amount of computing power, which would by then have been more useful if you just used it to mine more bitcoins.

The security system, aside from ensuring the reliability of Bitcoin transactions, also ensures that the identity of the Bitcoin users can be protected. Unlike in credit cards, your account number does not have any value in your transactions, which are ultimately verified using a private and public key.

It works like this: you put a digital signature to your transactions using your private key which can be verified by the users of the network using your public key. The keys are encrypted so that the public key can only ever work if you had used the correct private key in the first place.

This means that:

1. Your identity can't be stolen by criminals to make fraudulent transactions in your name.
2. You can choose to remain completely anonymous in the Bitcoin network, which may prove useful for some.

Lastly, bitcoins have the possibility of providing an ease of convenience that surpasses the traditional paying methods that we already have now. According to the Bitcoin site, using bitcoins allow you "to send and receive bitcoins anywhere in the world at any time.

No bank holidays. No borders. No bureaucracy. Bitcoin allows its users to be in full control of their money."

Bitcoins Are Incredibly Scarce

Fiat currency has a technically unlimited supply in the sense that governments can produce money whenever they want. Obviously, they don't do that because it will lead to inflation, so the production and release of money is controlled by the government based on intensive research on market trends and needs. Bitcoin, as you might have guessed, does not work the same.

Because Bitcoin is decentralized, there is no authority that decides when to make new bitcoins. The system is designed so that new bitcoins can only be created as part of a reward system for the miners.

And the reward is well-deserved: the backbone of the Bitcoin system is cryptography, or the art of writing and solving codes which requires a hefty amount of work to solve.

To update the blockchain, miners from all over the world have to race to solve a specific math problem called SHA-256, which stands for Secure Hash Algorithm 256 bit.

It's basically a math problem wherein you're given an output and you're supposed to find the input, like solving for x and y given that x + y = 2.

The only way to solve this kind of problem is through guesswork, and to solve the SHA-256, you'd have to go through an *insane* amount of possible solutions before you find the answer—for which you'd need an extremely powerful (not to mention expensive) computer.

Miners invest a lot of money on these supercomputers (as well as the huge amount of electricity it needs to run) all to mine new Bitcoins.

Jason Bloomberg, in an article for Forbes, writes that the value of Bitcoin is representative of this effort: because mining bitcoins take hard work, they become more valuable.So, first point to its scarcity is that bitcoins are hard to come by. You'd need a sizeable investment just to be able to create new bitcoins.

But they're even made scarcer due to the fact that there can only ever be a certain number of bitcoins in existence, which is 21 million. (If you're wondering why 21 million, it's basically because that's what's written in the source code.)

> *The cap on Bitcoin production is there to ensure that Bitcoin wouldn't ever be hyperinflated.*

It's even designed to be produced steadily: the reward system goes by half every 210,000 blocks added to the chain (i.e., every four years), with the SHA-256 problems even varying in difficulty depending on the amount of miners—more miners mean harder problems to ensure that not too many bitcoins get produced all at once.

Projecting from this trend, the last bitcoin is estimated to be mined around the year 2140. To put things in perspective, there are about 16.74 million bitcoins in existence at the time of writing.

That fewer and fewer bitcoins can be mined as time goes by drives up the interest of the people in the currency, because rarity is desirable and highly marketable.

This increases the value of Bitcoin, because it operates using a network—the larger the network, the greater use you can get out of Bitcoin.

Supply And Demand Affects Bitcoin Value Directly

The market value of Bitcoin—that is, the money that people are willing to pay for it—follows the same old basic demand and supply rule: a high demand increases its price and a low demand decreases it.

Before we go in any further, just remember that the value of something is not the same as its price; value is what people perceive a product is worth, while price is what they pay for it. Even so, value and price go hand in hand: the price of something is directly related to its value and vice versa.

According to an article in the Economist, the increasing trend in the price of Bitcoin is what drives people to invest in it.

People are investing because they believe that, following the trend so far, they would be able to sell their Bitcoins for a much higher price in the future—which the article argues is a perfect example of the greater-fool theory.

Basically, the greater-fool theory states that the price of a product is determined not by its intrinsic value, but by the beliefs and expectations that the consumers put on the product.

From this perspective, the surging price of Bitcoin serves not to increase its actual value, but to render it irrelevant.

The market is driving the price of Bitcoin up because of growing belief that it will be worth more in the future, not because they think its value is increasing over time. However, some people argue that the surge in Bitcoin prices that the past year has seen is not indicative of it being a bubble.

In the Bitcoin site itself, it argues that it is not a bubble, citing that bubbles are artificially overvaluations of a product which tends to correct itself eventually.

It cites its relatively small and young market as the reason for the volatility in Bitcoin prices—that "choices based on individual human action by hundreds of thousands of market participants is the cause for Bitcoin's price to fluctuate as the market seeks price discovery."

It argues that the volatility of Bitcoin prices are due to many forces such as:

- Loss of confidence in Bitcoin
- A large difference between value and price not based on the fundamentals of the Bitcoin economy
- Increased press coverage stimulating speculative demand
- Fear of uncertainty
- And old-fashioned irrational exuberance and greed

As such, Bitcoin is arguing that its growing prices can be attributed to more and more people finding the product increasingly worth their money based on its utility, thereby validating its value.

So, in summary: Bitcoin's utility and scarcity gives it value, but its prices seem to send opposing signals as to whether it's truly valuable or not.

With more and more people beginning to show interest in Bitcoin, perhaps we are barely scratching the surface of what its true value may be.

Different Techniques To Acquire Bitcoin

There are many different techniques to acquiring bitcoins, and in this guide, we will show you the most popular methods of getting yourself some units of the world's most popular cryptocurrency.

Buy Some Bitcoins

Buying bitcoins is a very simple and straightforward process. You can simply go to a bitcoin exchange website such as Coinbase or Kraken, and exchange your US Dollars, British Pounds, Euros, Canadian Dollars, and other supported currencies (this will depend on the platform) into some bitcoins.

Of course, with the ever-increasing value of bitcoin, this is easier said than done.

Right now, you can expect to shell out more than $10,000 for a single bitcoin! The good news is that you don't have to buy a whole bitcoin. Each bitcoin can be divided into 100 million units called Satoshis (named after Bitcoin founder, Satoshi Nakamoto).

This means you can buy a few thousand Satoshis for a few dollars. While this won't make you rich, you can at least get a feel for how bitcoins and cryptocurrency works.

Here are some of the best places where you can buy bitcoins:

Cryptocurrency Exchanges

There are plenty of platforms where you can buy and sell cryptocurrency. The most popular ones that have been around a few years are Coinbase, Kraken, Gemini, Coinmama, and CEX.io.

You'll have to do some research, however, if your state or country is supported and what currencies and payment methods they accept as each platform would have their own rules and regulations.

The transaction fees involved will also vary in each platform so you'll definitely have to look around to find the best cryptocurrency exchange that would suit your bitcoin needs.

Cash Exchanges

If you want to avoid bitcoin exchange platforms and pay directly in cash (or another payment method that's popular in your local area), use cash exchanges like LocalBitcoin or Wall of Coins. These platforms allow you to trade directly with another person.

There are no expensive transaction fees involved. However, they may charge a fee for successful trades. We would suggest that you look for a platform that offers an escrow service to make sure the seller doesn't run away with your hard-earned cash!

Trade Your Other Cryptocurrencies For Bitcoin

If you've got a digital wallet full of other cryptocurrencies, you can easily trade these for bitcoins. You can go to sites like ShapeShift.io which allows you to quickly trade your non-bitcoin cryptocurrency to bitcoins.

You don't even need an account to make a trade. Simply enter the amount you wish to convert or trade, your bitcoin address, and your cryptocurrency refund address. That's it! You'll have your new bitcoins in a few minutes.

Get Paid With Bitcoins

Getting paid with bitcoins is not a complicated process at all. You simply need to have your own bitcoin wallet so you can start receiving payments. For starters, you can create a free online wallet on Blockchain.info or Coinbase.

All you need is a valid email address to sign up and begin receiving payments! Once your wallet is set up, you can either generate a QR code or use the long alphanumeric address and send it to the person you wish to receive bitcoins from.

Here are some ideas on how you can get paid with bitcoins:

Work For Bitcoins

There are many different types of work you can do to get paid in bitcoin. It doesn't matter if you work online or offline as making and receiving bitcoin payments is so simple you don't really need technical know-how to do it.

Solopreneurs find this payment method so much more convenient as they don't need to wait 24-48 hours (or more for international workers) to receive bank transfers from their clients. They can receive their payment, salary, or wages in just a few minutes.

It's a big relief to workers knowing they don't need to wait in limbo, unsure if they're going to get paid for their hard work or not. Employers or clients also like the idea of not paying those exorbitant bank fees for doing transfers especially to workers or freelancers overseas.

> *With bitcoin payments, they get to save plenty of money just in bank fees alone!*

Sell Products Or Services

Whether you are an online shop or a brick-and-mortar store, you can choose to receive payments in bitcoin. With a growing community of bitcoin users, you're bound to get new and repeat customers who will do business with you simply because you're forward-thinking enough to accept bitcoin payments.

The added benefit to customers is they can easily send you payments straight from their bitcoin wallets while you receive their payments almost instantly. It's really a win-win situation for both you and your customers!

For online shops, you can use plugins or scripts to start accepting bitcoin payments on your site. If you're unsure of how you can do this, it's best to hire a developer to make sure it's set up right (you don't want those bitcoin payments going somewhere else!).

When your customers go to your checkout page, they'll see the bitcoin option and select that if they want to pay using bitcoins.

For local shops like hotels, restaurants, bars, cafes, flower shops, groceries, etc., if you want to receive bitcoin payments in person, all you have to do is just print your wallet's QR code and pin it near your cash register.

When your customers are ready to pay, simply direct them to the QR code, have them scan it on their mobile phones, enter the amount they need to pay, hit Send, and wait for your bitcoins to arrive.

Oh, and don't forget to add a giant 'Bitcoin Accepted Here' sign at the entrance to invite the bitcoin community to come inside! To attract even more bitcoin users, add your business to Coinmap and other similar sites where the bitcoin community hangs out and searches for places where they can spend their bitcoins!

Receive Tips From Customers

You don't need to be in the service industry to receive tips. If you have a blog, you can set up a bitcoin payment gateway where your loyal fans and readers can tip you if they so desire.

Don't underestimate the generosity of your audience especially if you produce content that provides a lot of value to them. Try it out – you just might be surprised to see some bitcoins on your wallet after a few days!

Complete Small Tasks On Websites

There are now plenty of sites on the Internet that offer free bitcoins (usually just a very, very small fraction of it) for every task you complete. Some websites require you to complete surveys, watch videos, click on ads, answer questions, sign up for trial offers, download mobile apps, play online games, refer friends, shop online, and more. Payment is usually quick and easy.

Some platforms just require your bitcoin wallet address while others require you to sign up and create an account. While it's true these jobs are mostly small and can be done in a few minutes, earning only a few hundred or thousand Satoshis at a time may not be worth it especially if you value your time. But if you've got nothing better to do and you want to experience first-hand the joys of owning cryptocurrency, then you've got plenty of micro-tasking sites to choose from.

Join Bitcoin Faucets

Bitcoin faucets are just websites that give away free Satoshis at set time intervals. These sites bring in a huge amount of traffic from people wanting to get free bitcoins so expect lots of competition and, depending on where the faucet is hosted, slow loading times.

Some faucets give away Satoshis with no work involved, that is, you just need to have the site up on your browser, while some require you to solve little tasks before you earn your Satoshis (much like the micro-tasking websites we've discussed in the previous section).

Sites like these are a major time drain as well so it's really up to you if you can afford to exchange your precious time for a few Satoshis.

Mine Your Own Bitcoin

Bitcoin miners play an extremely important role in the Bitcoin network. Without miners, there would be no new bitcoins, and no transactions would be confirmed. Bitcoin miners are so important to the Bitcoin ecosystem that they are justly rewarded with bitcoins for their hard work. However, bitcoin mining is not as profitable as it seems.

When Bitcoin was still in its infancy, miners were getting paid 50 bitcoins for every block mined. But every 210,000 blocks (this is around 4 years), the reward is halved. So this means that the initial 50 bitcoins was halved into 25 bitcoins.

And now, at this particular point in time, the block reward is down to 12.5 bitcoins. If you consider the price for one bitcoin right now (well over $10,000), this is still is a very attractive reward indeed. And experts predict the price will continue to go up as the number of bitcoins in existence slowly go up, too, and the demand for more bitcoins continue to increase.

Mining bitcoins is not an easy job, much like any other physical mining job in the real world. Bitcoin miners may not get dirty from soot and mud, but their powerful computers do.

The difficulty in mining new blocks has gone up so much that individual miners are finding it extremely difficult to solve complex cryptographic functions on their own. Many different miners or mining groups compete to discover a new block and the mining difficulty are at extremely high levels now.

Most, if not all, miners are forced to work in mining pools where several miners work together as a group to add new transactions to the blockchain. When a new block is mined, the reward is split according to the work each miner's computer has done.

Mining bitcoins doesn't come cheap. You can't just use any computer as solving cryptographic functions will take so much of your computer's processing power.

Not even a high-end laptop or desktop computer can do the job anymore – it's really that difficult to mine new bitcoin blocks today!

Even if you join mining pools, you'll need to invest a lot of money to buy the right hardware. In the beginning, a powerful CPU (Computer Processing Unit) and GPU (Graphical Processing Unit) were sufficient to mine new blocks. However, as the difficulty of mining bitcoins have gone up, more processing power was needed.

Today, an ASIC (Application Specific Integrated Circuit) chip is seen as the only way to succeed in mining. A bitcoin-mining ASIC chip is designed specifically to mine bitcoins. It can't do any other task apart from mining bitcoins.

While this may be viewed as a downside for some, remember that mining is a hard job. You need all the resources you can use to find the next transaction block so you can add it to the blockchain and get rewarded bitcoins in the process. Professional miners find this hardware very powerful than other technologies used in the past.

Also, it's not as power hungry as other hardware out there. It will still consume plenty of power, however, so consider that if you're worried about your electricity bills.

If you are prepared to buy the technology to mine bitcoins as well as pay more costly power bills, then mining bitcoins will be a great way for you to acquire this particular cryptocurrency.

However, we'd like to say that this is not a job for the uninitiated. It's best to leave this task to the experts or those with an in-depth knowledge of how bitcoin mining works. As we've shown you in this guide, there are many ways you can acquire bitcoins that don't require a healthy investment of both time and money.

In the next chapter, we'll go into more detail on bitcoin mining, and you'll see for yourself if this is something you want to get involved in.

Bitcoin Mining – Everything You Need To Know About Bitcoin Mining

In this guide, we'll cover everything there is to know about Bitcoin mining so you can find out if this is something that you would like to do so you can get your fair share of bitcoins.

Bitcoin has been in the news a lot nowadays, and its current price is a source of interest to a lot of people around the world. A few years ago, many people labeled Bitcoin as a scam, but now it is seen, along with other cryptocurrencies, as the future of money.

> *Cryptocurrencies, as virtual or digital currencies, have no physical properties and need to be 'mined' electronically.*

Before we go into details, we'd like to define first the most common terms used in Bitcoin mining so you can easily understand how this highly technical process works.

Bitcoin Mining Terms You Should Get To Know

Block: The data related to transactions is stored on a page known as a block.

Bitcoins Per Block: This is the number of bitcoins rewarded to miners for every block mined and added to the blockchain. The initial reward per block was 50 bitcoins but every 210,000 blocks, the reward is divided by 2. Currently, the reward sits at 12.5 bitcoins per block.

Bitcoin Difficulty: With an increasing number of miners, Bitcoin mining also increases in difficulty. The ideal average mining time defined by the network is 10 minutes per block.

Electricity Rate: To calculate how much you're earning, you need to check your electric bill. This can help you judge how much electricity is consumed by your mining computer in return for your bitcoin earnings. Are you making a profit, breaking even or losing? These are important questions all miners need to ask themselves.

Hash: In Bitcoin mining, a hash can be seen as a problem related to mathematics. The mining machine needs to solve it to earn rewards.

Hash Rate: The time it takes to solve these hash problems is called Hash Rate. Hash rate increases with the number of miners on the Bitcoin network. MH/s (Mega hash per second), GH/s (Giga hash per second), TH/s (Terra hash per second) and PH/s (Peta hash per second) are some of the units that are used in measuring hash rates.

Pool Fees: Miners join a pool for mining known as a 'mining pool.' Like natural mining, miners here mine together as it helps them solve those complex hash problems faster. You have to pay fees to the pool so it can continue its operations. When bitcoins are finally mined, they are distributed to miners with respect to their hash rates.

Power Consumption: Not every mining machine consumes the same amount of electricity. So before buying yourself an expensive machine, you must check first how much power it will consume.

Time Frame: This is a duration that you need to define yourself to see how much you're mining. For example, you define a time frame of 45 days. This means that after 45 days, you'll calculate how many bitcoins you've mined during this period. Defining a time frame can help you see if you are producing more or less than your fellow miners.

Bitcoin Mining Hardware Commonly Used By Miners

CPU (Computer Processing Unit):

In the beginning, bitcoin mining was incredibly easy and could be easily mined on regular desktop CPUs. However, as the number of miners increased, bitcoin mining on CPU became more difficult and caused computer hard drives to fail.

GPU (Graphical Processing Unit):

With a surge in the number of miners on the network, the use of GPUs started to gain popularity when people realized they were more efficient for bitcoin mining.

Some advanced GPUs even allowed miners to increase their mining productivity 50-100 times better in comparison to CPU mining. People also started altering their BIOS settings to maximize their rewards. Nvidia and ATI's cards shot to popularity as a result.

FPGA (Field-Programmable Gate Array):

FPGA is an integrated circuit created with the objective of performing bitcoin mining. GPU mining was turning out to be not so profitable for everyone because of rising electricity costs. FPGA was designed to consume less power, and so miners moved from GPUs to FPGAs.

ASIC (Application-Specific Integrated Circuit):

With the arrival of ASIC technology, FPGA was overtaken as the primary hardware used in bitcoin mining. ASIC is a computer chip that is used solely for mining of cryptocurrencies like bitcoins or other coins that use the SHA-256 algorithm.

Unlike other mining hardware, ASICs cannot be used to do tasks other than mining. Right now, this is the gold standard which miners swear by as these powerful chips solve more problems in less time while consuming less electricity as well.

The Role Of Mining In The Creation Of New Bitcoins

You can own bitcoins using a few methods. The easiest way is to buy some bitcoins on a Bitcoin exchange platform though, of course, bitcoin prices are so high now that you'll need to make a sizeable investment.

The other method is not to use any money and instead simply mine bitcoins using computer hardware.

It's important to note here that the main and integral purpose of mining is the creation or release of new bitcoins which can be then available on the network.

Currently, about 16 million bitcoins have already been mined out of the possible 21 million bitcoins that can ever be created.

What Is The Blockchain?

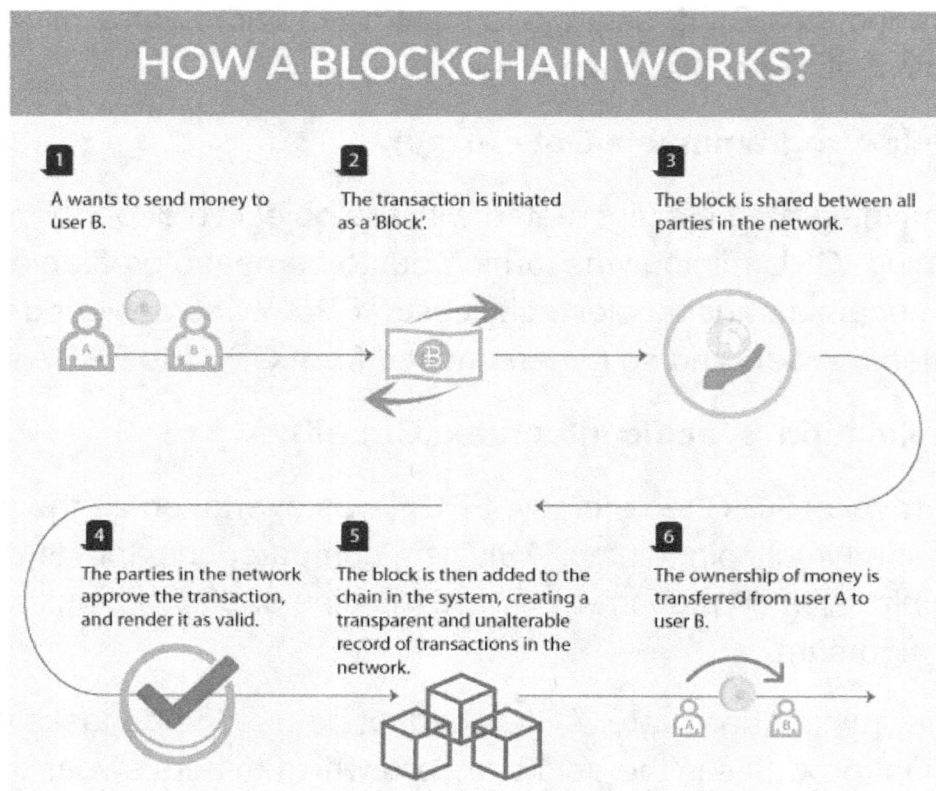

(Image Source: Biz2Credit)

Unlike normal currency transactions being confirmed and regulated through banks, cryptocurrencies' transactional data appears a public ledger known as the 'blockchain'.

Each block can be said as a page that contains the data of transactions. That is why it is called as blockchain. Mining helps to confirm these transactions on a blockchain.

Miners also run cryptographic hash on blocks. A hash requires complex computations.

These hashes are important because they make a block secure. Once a block has been accepted in the blockchain then it can't be altered. Miners anonymously validate these transactions.

For their help, miners are rewarded bitcoins. 'Proof of work' is the term coined for the assistance of miners in validating transactions.

What Exactly Is Bitcoin Mining?

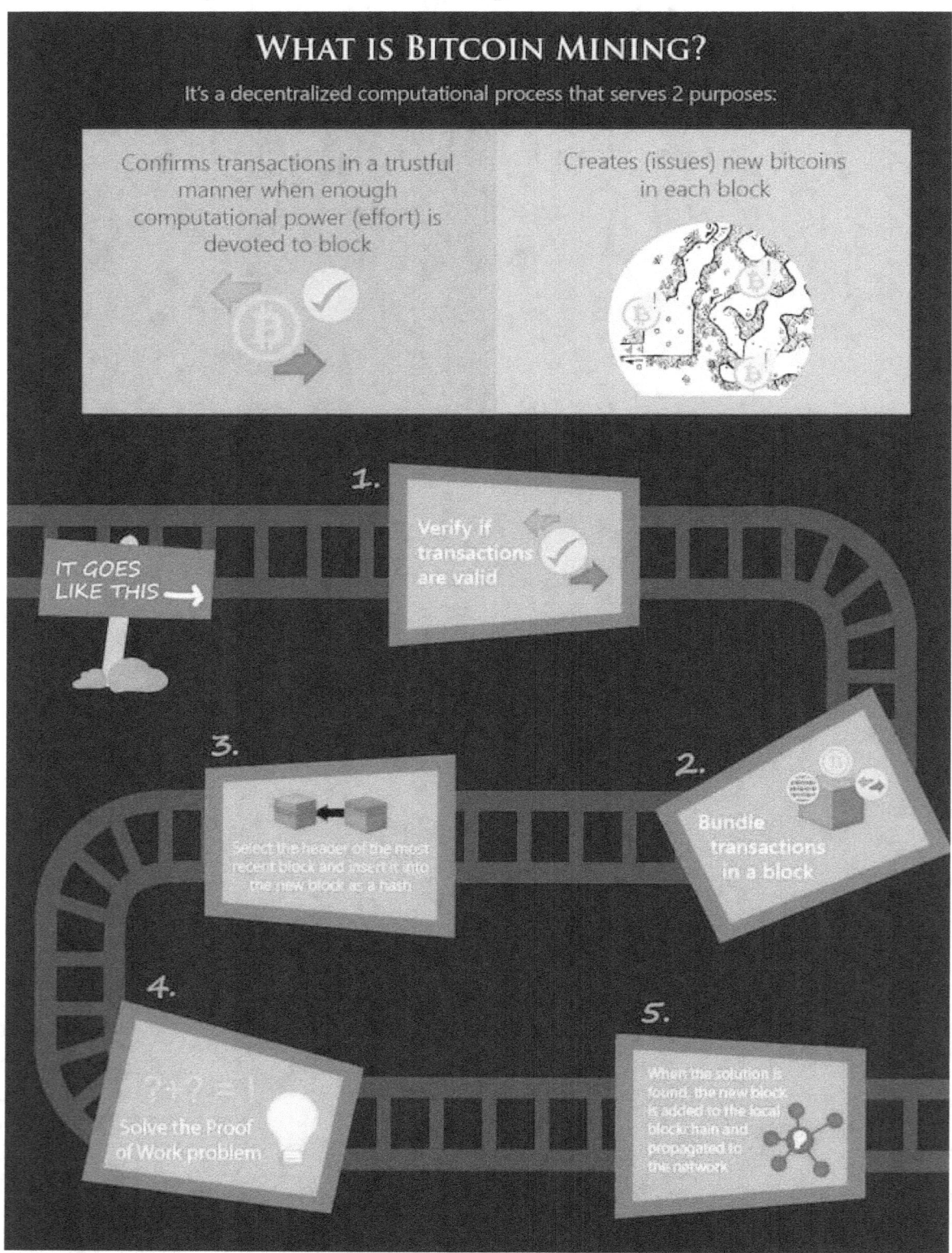

(Image Source: BitcoinMining.com)

The term 'mining' is often used with natural resources like gold, silver, and other minerals. These resources are limited in supply and are therefore very valuable commodities, much like Bitcoin.

Similarly, 'mining' is the term used by Bitcoin founder, Satoshi Nakamoto, because miners will essentially be going deep into the Bitcoin network to mine those precious coins.

Bitcoin miners may not get dirty on their hands and knees to mine bitcoins, but with the increasing difficulty of solving complex cryptographic hash functions, they might as well be!

The Bitcoin mining process creates these 2 results: the first is it secures and verifies transactions that are happening on the Bitcoin network, and the second is it creates new bitcoins.

Bitcoin mining involves using the SHA-256 algorithm. SHA stands for Secure Hashing Algorithm which is a computational algorithm that is used for encryption.

Since Bitcoin is a decentralized type of currency, meaning no central body or authority gives permissions to miners, anyone with access to electricity and a mining machine can mine bitcoin.

However, these mining machines are themselves very costly as you need specialized computer chips to mine bitcoin efficiently, as those complex hash functions miners need to solve become more complicated over time.

In the early days, you could use your computer's CPU (computer processing unit) and GPU (graphics processing unit) to solve hash problems, but today the problems are so complicated, miners are setting up expensive rigs and forming mining groups to pool their computer resources!

Individual miners are left with no choice but to join mining groups because their individual machines just cannot handle the difficult workload.

Bitcoin Mining And Mining Difficulty

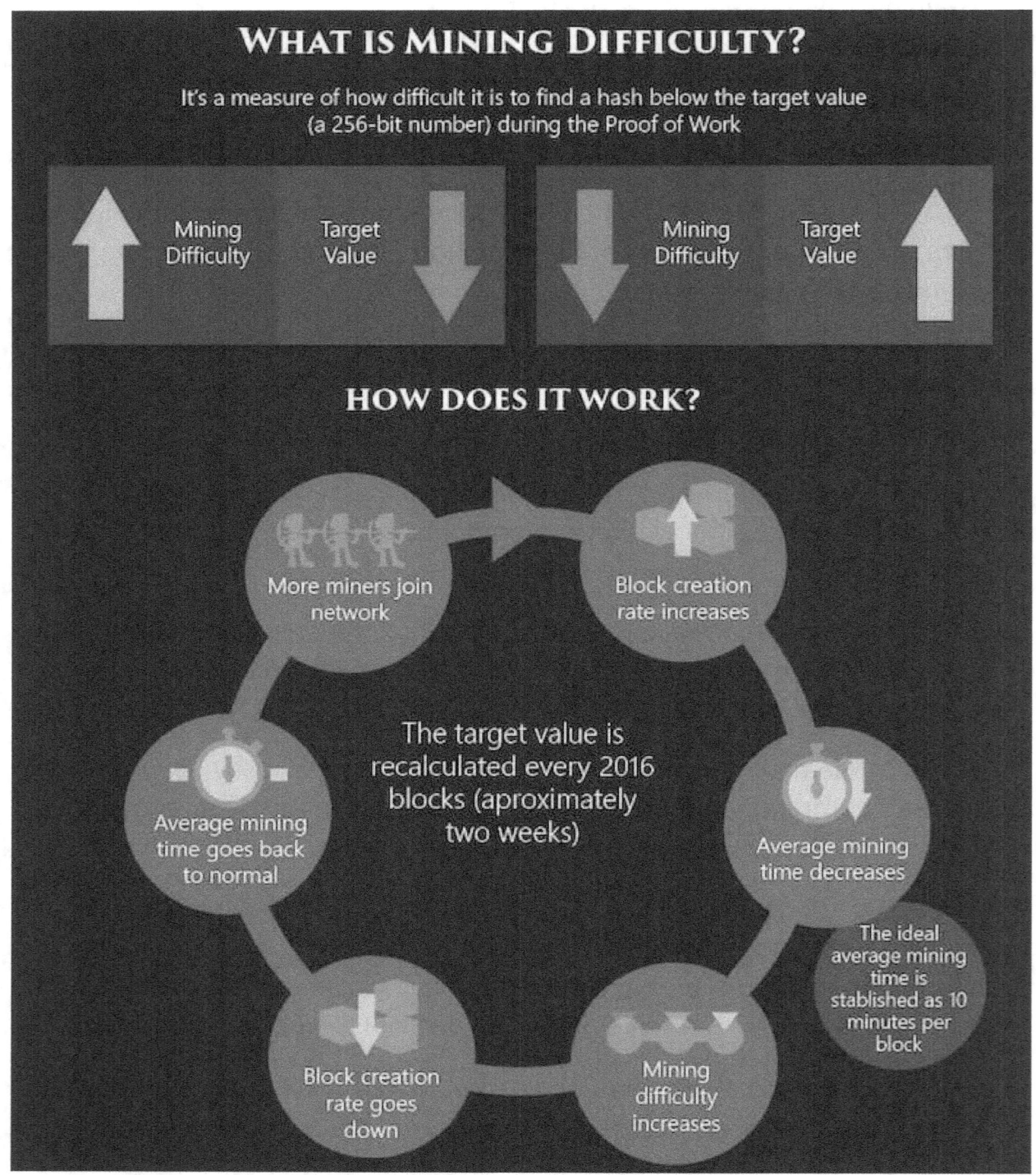

(Image Source: BitcoinMining.com)

Computers involved in bitcoin mining try to solve complex mathematical problems that are near impossible for a human being to solve. Not only are these problems becoming increasingly difficult, but they are also time-consuming for computers as these take a lot of time, and electric power, to solve.

In fact, expert miners estimate that approximately $150,000 worth of electricity is used each day by Bitcoin miners all over the world!

On average, it takes about 10 minutes for Bitcoin miners to find a new block with each block containing about 2,000 transactions. These 10 minutes is the time needed for bitcoin transactions to be validated by the network and to form a new block.

Hence, a new block is created every time these complex problems get solved. This process is more commonly known as 'Proof Of Work,' and this eliminates the possibility of having only a few miners mine all the remaining bitcoins for themselves.

Since Bitcoin's network is decentralized without a central body verifying the transactions, this self-governed system means each miner is an integral part of the system. Without miners, there would be no bitcoins, plain and simple. Due to the important role miners' play in the Bitcoin network, they are rewarded in a few ways.

First, the transaction fees that users pay for each bitcoin transaction is sent to the miners. Secondly, the network rewards each winning miner a set number of bitcoins; the second reward is important because this is the only way that new bitcoins are created. Thus, miners have to continue mining so that more bitcoins are created and released into the network.

In 2009, when the first Bitcoin block was mined by Satoshi Nakamoto himself, the reward was 50 bitcoins for each block. However, the reward is reduced by half every 210,000 blocks or approximately 4 years.

This means that 210,000 blocks after the genesis (or first ever) block was mined, the miner who successfully mined the 210,001st block was only rewarded 25 bitcoins; this occurred on 28th November 2012.

Then another 210,000 blocks later, on 9th July 2016, the reward was again halved, this time into 12.5 bitcoins. It is expected that sometime in the year 2021, the next 210,000 blocks will be completed and the reward will drop down to 6.25 bitcoins.

Another interesting thing to note is that while the rewards are getting smaller and smaller, the mining difficulty is increasing. There's far more competition now, and solo miners find it near to impossible to find a single block by themselves. Joining mining groups allow several miners to pool their resources, but this also means they are sharing the bitcoin reward among themselves.

Bitcoin Cloud Mining – An Alternative To Joining Mining Pools?

Beware! Bitcoin cloud mining platforms are full of Ponzi-style scamming operations. While some see this as a great alternative to mining pools, there are only a few legitimate cloud mining operations.

In theory, cloud mining is the perfect solution to people who want to mine bitcoins without buying their own mining computers and joining a pool.

They don't need to worry about electricity and all the other problems that real miners have to deal with. In short, all you have to do is pay up the subscription fee and wait for your bitcoin earnings to be sent to your wallet. Sounds great, right?

Many people are attracted to this model, and of course, scammers and thieves are ready to lend them a hand and relieve them of their money.

Is Bitcoin Mining Profitable?

This million dollar question will get you many different answers. Some would encourage you to go ahead and mine, while others will tell you the time to mine bitcoins has passed. With Bitcoin prices continuously breaking records and reaching all-time highs, the investment may be worth it.

But Bitcoin is such a volatile cryptocurrency, and we can never predict the direction its price is going to take, so it's a huge risk for miners as well when the price drops.

When this happens, the best thing for miners to do is to hold on to their bitcoins and wait for the price to go back up again before selling their bitcoins to eager buyers.

Bitcoin Storing – How To Store Your Bitcoin And Other Cryptocurrency Safely

Keeping your bitcoins safe from prying eyes, malicious bots, hackers and your garden-variety thieves, is not easy. Everyone wants a piece of bitcoin nowadays, it seems.

If people know you've invested in Bitcoin in the early days, and you still have your investment with you, then they know you're literally sitting on top of a fortune. We don't want to sound sinister, but it's just sad a fact of life that some people will do anything for money or in this case, bitcoins.

There are many ways you can keep your precious digital fortune safe. Just like your paper money, you can store different amounts of bitcoin in different types of wallets. Some are 'hot' wallets while some are considered 'cold.' You'll learn more about these types of wallets as we go through each of them in this guide.

It's important to mention here that when we say 'keeping the bitcoins safe,' we're actually referring to keeping the 'private key' safe. Within your wallet, your bitcoins would have an associated address, and each bitcoin address is composed of a 'public key' and a 'private key.'

The public key is THE bitcoin address itself, and it can be shared with anybody. The public key can be compared to an email address. Everybody who knows your email address can send you emails.

The private key is analogous to your email password. Without a password, no one can read your email. In the same way, without a private key, you can't make a transaction to send bitcoins to another user. This is why keeping the private key safe is of utmost importance.

If hackers get hold of your private key, they can send ALL your bitcoins to their own accounts.

Because of the way Bitcoin is designed, there's no way for you to know where your bitcoins would be sent and there is absolutely zero chance of retrieving any bitcoins. Bitcoin's most attractive features such as near-instant transfers, anonymous and irreversible transactions are also your biggest concerns if your private keys get stolen.

Once your bitcoins are stolen and transferred to another user, you really have no other choice but to accept the fact and move on. There is nothing else you can do.

So let's move on to how you can keep your private keys, and your bitcoins, safe from hackers and thieves.

Online Wallets

The easiest way to get started with bitcoins is by getting an online wallet. You don't even need to have bitcoins yet to get your own wallet. You can simply go to sites like Blockchain.info, Coinbase.com, and other bitcoin exchange platforms to create your first wallet.

Online or web wallets are great for those just getting their feet wet with bitcoins and those who don't have a sizeable inventory of bitcoins yet.

They are easy to setup, they're very convenient, and you can access them from anywhere with an Internet connection. Online wallets are 'hot wallets' for this very reason – anyone can access your wallet, too!

In fact, what's even worse is that most web wallets store your private keys on their servers so if the platform is hacked, then your bitcoins are as good as gone.

Likewise, if a serious technical glitch happens on the site, your private keys could be compromised or totally gone. There's also the very real threat of having your account limited or suspended by the platform. You may unknowingly go against the site's terms of service or something similar, and they can shut your account down, and your private keys, forever.

If you've got a significant bitcoin stash, then it's best if you move it to a more secure 'cold' wallet that's not connected to the Internet. Not having control over your bitcoins is a scary thought and one that you shouldn't take a chance on.

While there are inherent risks to online wallets, it's not all bad especially if you make transactions frequently. You can just store a few bitcoins in your online wallet for those regular transactions and keep the rest in a more secure wallet.

This way you'll still get to experience the convenience of an online wallet while having peace of mind that a large percentage of your bitcoins are out of harm's way.

Mobile Wallets

Just like online wallets, mobile app wallets are also 'hot' wallets because you can easily access your bitcoins anywhere you've got an Internet connection. Out of all the wallets on this guide, mobile wallets are the most convenient. It may not be the safest, but no one can deny its convenience.

You can send bitcoin payments to any merchant online or offline. Some web wallets have a mobile counterpart. For instance, both Blockchain.info and Coinbase mobile wallets are synced to your web wallets which is really very convenient as both wallets sync automatically so you can see your balance when you log in or access either wallet.

This convenience is precisely why more local businesses should accept bitcoin payments. The Bitcoin community is growing at an exponential rate, and these savvy users would be installing mobile wallets on their iPhones and Android smartphones.

There's probably no easier way for them to pay than just scanning your bitcoin address' QR code and hitting that Send button to pay for your products or services!

However, not everything is good with mobile wallets. For instance, your private keys can still be accessed by hackers whether it's saved on a third party server or your mobile phone.

If you lose your mobile device or it gets damaged, you could also potentially lose all your bitcoins and other cryptocurrency if you didn't make backup copies of your private keys and stored them somewhere safe.

The best way to take advantage of a mobile wallet is by only transferring what you need from a more secure wallet (like a hardware wallet) to your mobile wallet. This way even if you lose your phone, and you can't recover your private keys on there, then you won't be losing all your bitcoins.

Desktop Wallet

The third type of wallet you can use to store your bitcoins relatively safely is a desktop wallet. It's basically a desktop app where you store your private keys in. The most popular one, though not always the most practical one, is Bitcoin Core.

When you install the software, you need to make sure you have more than 150GB (or more) free disk space as it will automatically download the entire blockchain dating back to 2009!

You can't not download the blockchain as Bitcoin Core will not process any transaction unless the entire ledger has been downloaded to your system. Once it's been downloaded, you can then start sending and receiving bitcoins to your wallet.

If you don't have plenty of disk space to spare, nor the bandwidth to download such a massive file, then here's some good news for you -- Bitcoin Core is not the only desktop wallet available nowadays.

You've actually got plenty of choices to choose from such as Electrum, Bither, Armory, and more, which don't require you to download the blockchain as it uses SPV (Simple Payment Verification) technology.

Desktop wallets are relatively easy to use, and it's safer than a web or mobile wallet because you can just disconnect your computer from the Internet to avoid hackers from getting in your system and stealing your private keys.

Of course, it's not as convenient as a web or mobile wallet, but at least you have full control over your private keys. You can keep a backup copy of the keys just in case your computer gets stolen, infected with a virus or permanently damaged.

> *If you don't backup your private keys, you could lose all your bitcoins in the blink of an eye.*

Paper Wallet

It might sound weird at first to store your digital cryptocurrency in a paper wallet. You're probably going to ask why anyone would do that when bitcoin doesn't exist physically.

Bitcoin and paper may not seem like a match made in heaven, but when you think about it, they actually do. Well, on some level at least.

Paper wallets are a form of 'cold storage' because Internet hackers won't ever get to hack into your little piece of paper. There are plenty of skilled hackers who can find a way to access most computers and servers, but we're pretty sure paper isn't one of them.

Your bitcoins may be safe from hackers but not from offline thieves. If you don't take care of your paper wallet, if you leave it lying around in unsecured places, then you're literally giving someone the keys to your fortune!

Water is also something you should consider when using paper wallets. Storing your wallets in zip locks and other water resistant containers should help overcome this problem.

Paper wallets are not as convenient as mobile or web wallets, but they are definitely more secure. You can print both your public and private keys and hide it somewhere safe like a safety deposit box.

> *Paper wallets are the best type of wallet for storing your private keys for long periods of time.*

If you don't intend to touch your bitcoins for months or years, then you can create paper wallets. Of course, just like we've recommended in previous sections, it's best to keep a few bitcoins (only what you can afford to lose) in more convenient wallets so you can continue sending and receiving bitcoins. The rest of your private keys can go in the paper wallet.

Hardware Wallet

There's a consensus in the Bitcoin community that hardware wallets are the safest bitcoin wallets and something every serious Bitcoin investor and enthusiast should consider buying. Unlike the other wallet types we've covered so far in this guide, hardware wallets are relatively expensive.

Of course, if you've got a considerable number of bitcoins to protect, then it's really a small price to pay for keeping your fortune safe. Most hardware wallets support a host of cryptocurrencies so if you've invested in non-bitcoin currencies too, then you'll find this type of wallet to be an excellent purchase.

Hardware wallets are basically powerful and durable USB sticks which you plug into your computer when making a bitcoin or cryptocurrency transaction. When you're done, simply remove the wallet and store it somewhere safe.

A unique security feature on hardware wallets is the ability to generate private keys offline which means that it's less vulnerable to hacker attacks. These sturdy little devices allow you to bring your private keys anywhere with you without fear of having it exposed to the outside world.

Setup is also quick and easy with hardware wallets. Depending on the wallet, you can assign a PIN code, password, or recovery seed words which you can use to authenticate your access as well as recover your bitcoins in case your wallet is lost or destroyed.

Just in case you get some form of amnesia and forget your recovery details, you should write down your secret details and hide it somewhere only you know. Otherwise, if someone finds it, either by accident or by design, then your bitcoins and whatever cryptocurrency you have on there will soon be gone.

Hardware wallets are excellent for storing all your cryptocurrencies safely. Whether you've got a sizeable collection of digital currency or not, you never have to worry if your wallet will be hacked and your money stolen.

Your private keys are relatively safe. You just need to make sure your memory never fails you, and you'll always remember where you've hidden your wallet backups!

To sum up this guide, the best wallet for your bitcoins and cryptocurrencies are actually a combination of different wallets. Use hard wallets or paper wallets for long-term storage, desktop wallets for medium-term storage, and web and mobile wallets for short-term storage and frequent transactions.

Trading And Selling Your Bitcoin For Profit

Trading and selling your bitcoin can be a very profitable activity. You probably know someone or heard about someone who bought bitcoins in the early days when they were worth almost nothing, and ended up selling each bitcoin for thousands of dollars!

Or you may know people who engage in trading bitcoins and are profiting very nicely as well. It might seem easy, but the truth is, trading bitcoins is not for everyone.

Beginners are especially advised to take caution and to be mentally and financially ready before taking the plunge into this exciting high-risk and high-reward world. When trading, it's common sense to follow the 'buy low and sell high' strategy so you can make a profit.

You don't want to sell at a price lower than when you bought in because you'll be selling at a loss. But all these sounds easy on paper.

In the real world, when you're dealing with bitcoins that's worth hundreds, thousands or even millions of dollars, if you don't have the right mindset and the financial discipline, you could panic very easily.

Especially if you're trading bitcoins that represent your entire life savings, your retirement fund, or your kids' college tuition!

Bitcoin Trading Strategies

Common sense and self-control should take precedence over greed and the idea of profiting thousands of dollars in a single day. Here are some bitcoin trading strategies to guide you in the trading world.

Practice First

Learning the ins and outs of bitcoin trading is great, but knowing just theory is different from real-world application. Some bitcoin exchanges offer a demo account where you can play around and experience real-world trading using real-time prices.

You'll get a feel for the landscape, so to speak, and you'll see for yourself whether you've got the stomach for the high-risk game of bitcoin trading.

Plan Your Strategy

To trade bitcoins successfully, you need to have a good strategy in place. You don't just blindly follow the news and think that because everyone's buying bitcoins, then you should be buying too.

Have a plan in place on what price you should buy bitcoins at and what price to sell them at to profit, and make sure you stick to that plan. This means keeping your panic at bay whenever you see the price drop.

Invest Small Amounts

As part of your practice or training strategy, you should start small and don't go all in when you first trade. It is fine to lose all your 'money' in a demo account, but when it's real money, you don't want to risk losing huge sums on your first day.

Control Your Emotions

It's normal to feel alarmed at the first hint of losing your money. However, as you already know Bitcoin is very volatile, and in a single day, the price can go down by hundreds or thousands of dollars. But the opposite is also true. The price can just as easily go up in the next hour or so.

> *If you keep your emotions in check and think logically, you too can make serious money with Bitcoin trading.*

However, if you fail to control your emotions and you let your panic overcome you, then you're bound to lose.

Popular Bitcoin Trading Platforms

Now that you know some very useful Bitcoin trading strategies, it's time to learn about some of the most popular trading platforms for Bitcoin and other cryptocurrencies.

Coinbase

Coinbase is one of the biggest digital currency exchanges in the world today with over 50 billion dollars' worth of digital currency exchanged since 2011. They currently serve more than 10 million customers based in 32 countries.

The platform is very easy to use, and you can easily buy and trade your digital currency.

- To begin, you have to create a free digital wallet which you can use to store your cryptocurrency.

- Next, you need to link your bank account, credit or debit card, so that you can exchange your local currency into the cryptocurrency of your choice.
- Once your account is set up and funded, it's time to buy some crypto.

You have the option to buy bitcoins, ethereum, and litecoin. You can do this either on their website or their handy mobile app.

Now that you've got some bitcoins, you can choose to start trading on Coinbase's GDAX (Global Digital Asset Exchange) trading platform although this is geared towards more advanced and experienced traders.

For beginners though, it's best to stick to Coinbase's more newbie-friendly interface. The good thing about Coinbase is that your digital currency is fully insured while your fiat currency (local currency) are stored in custodial bank accounts. The USD Coinbase wallets of US citizens are covered by FDIC insurance, up to a maximum of $250,000.

To sell your bitcoins, ethereum or litecoins, you simply need to indicate the amount you want to sell and the wallet you're selling from. Then select the linked bank account you wish to deposit your cash to.

At this time, Coinbase does not allow the proceeds of your sale to be sent to a credit or debit card, so it's important you link a bank account to your Coinbase account.

Kraken

Kraken is one of the most trusted names in bitcoin and cryptocurrency exchange since 2011. The company is also considered to be the largest bitcoin exchange in terms of Euro volume and liquidity. In addition to trading bitcoins, they also trade US dollars, Canadian dollars, British pounds and Japanese yen.

Many international users love Kraken because it's very accessible internationally and they support many different types of national currencies and cryptocurrencies.

Kraken offers many options for trading. You can easily trade between any of their 17 supported cryptocurrencies with Euros, USD, CAD, JPY, and GBP. They offer so many possible trading pairs, they have a very long page dedicated just for their fee schedule!

To get started with Kraken, you need to create a free account. After you've verified your account, you can then fund it with cash or cryptocurrency and then place an order to buy bitcoins (or another crypto) on the exchange.

When your order request is fulfilled, you can then withdraw your bitcoins/crypto to your wallet. Their web interface is relatively simple when ordering, however, their trading tools are robust and are great for more advanced users.

To sell bitcoins, you need to send your bitcoins from your wallet to your Kraken account and then create a new order to sell or trade them for any of the available national currencies. Once your order is filled, you can then proceed to withdraw the cash to your linked bank account.

CEX.io

CEX.io is one of the most popular cryptocurrency exchange platforms today with over 1 million active users worldwide. However, the company wasn't originally an exchange; it was actually established in 2013 as the first ever cloud mining provider. While the mining aspect of the business has since been closed, their exchange platform is clearly thriving.

Many users appreciate CEX.io's pricing transparency. If you're buying bitcoins, they make it so easy for you to see how much your $100, $200, $500 or $1000 is going to get you. You can also easily see just how much bitcoin you can buy in British Pound, Euro, and Russian Ruble. The buying price is updated every 120 seconds.

To get started, you need to create an account and add funds to it by using your credit card (you can link any number of credit cards to your account), or you can do a bank transfer, too. They accept USD, EUR, RUB, GBP, or your local currency.

Once the funds are added to your account, you can easily buy bitcoins with 1 click. You then have the option of storing it in your CEX.io wallet, trade it or withdraw to your personal wallet.

Selling bitcoins is also very easy on CEX.io. Simply have the bitcoins in your account, then use their handy buy/sell section for instant cash, or you can place an order in the Trade section of the site (you might get a better exchange rate if you trade).

You can quickly withdraw your earnings to your Visa or Mastercard and receive your funds instantly. Alternatively, for larger transactions, you can withdraw via bank transfer or SEPA if you're in Europe.

Bitstamp

Founded in 2011 in the UK, Bitstamp is one of the pioneers in Bitcoin trading. They are constantly improving their services, and to date, they allow trading of bitcoin, ripple, litecoin, ether and bitcoin cash. Bitstamp has a good reputation worldwide especially since they accept trades from anyone in the world.

All major credit cards are accepted as well, so it makes the platform very friendly to international users. They also promise no hidden fees with transparent volume-based pricing. They guarantee that 98% of digital funds are stored offline for security.

Bitstamp does not sell bitcoins themselves. Instead, they provide a service or platform where people trade directly with each other and buyers get their bitcoins and sellers get their cash at the price they want.

To get started with buying and selling bitcoins, you must create a Bitstamp account. You then need to transfer funds to your account via SEPA, wire transfer or credit card. Once payment is credited, you can place an instant buy order which will allow you to automatically buy bitcoins at the lowest price offered on the Bitstamp market.

A second option to buy bitcoins is by placing a limit order wherein you can set the price you are willing to buy bitcoins.

To sell bitcoins, you need to load your Bitstamp account with bitcoins first. Once you've done this, you can then place an instant sell order to automatically sell your bitcoins at the highest price offered on the market.

Alternatively, you can place a sell limit order where you can set the price at which you are willing to sell your bitcoins. Once your bitcoins are sold, you can proceed to withdraw your funds in USD or EUR currency.

Bitfinex

Since 2014, Hong Kong-based Bitfinex has been the world's largest cryptocurrency trading platform in terms of volume. This full-featured spot trading platform allows trades among the major cryptocurrencies such as Bitcoin, Ethereum, Litecoin, Money, Dash, Ripple, and more. Having such a large volume of Bitcoin exchanges happening on this platform implies the best liquidity.

This means you can trade a large volume of bitcoins at the price you want. Bitfinex's fees are also very low as compared to other cryptocurrency exchanges on this guide. This is why a lot of people like trading on this platform as more money goes to their accounts instead of being paid in fees.

Funding your Bitfinex account is not as simple as the other exchanges though. The only way to deposit money is via bank wire transfer which can take days. On top of the delay, you'd also have to pay Bitfinex a 0.1% of the deposit amount with a $20 minimum. Withdrawing your dollars is also a headache as they only offer bank wire withdrawals. Your money may take up to 7 days to post to your account!

To avoid this inconvenience, trading experts suggest getting your bitcoins or other crypto elsewhere and then just transferring it to your Bitfinex account. For withdrawals, you can withdraw your crypto to your wallet and then sell it locally. This workaround means you just use Bitfinex strictly for trading cryptocurrencies.

Are You Ready To Start Trading Bitcoins?

There are many more bitcoin and cryptocurrency exchanges we've not been able to include in this guide. It's best to perform due diligence and research before selecting a trading platform. Just remember that whichever cryptocurrency exchange platform you choose to do business with, you must always move your cryptocurrency to a more secure wallet such as a hardware wallet or paper wallet.

Don't leave it in your exchange's wallet as it's at great risk of being stolen by hackers. If you must store some in your online wallet, just keep the smallest amount you can afford to lose.

Using Bitcoin As An Investment Strategy

Bitcoin is a relatively new form of currency which is just starting to gain traction and worldwide acceptance. With the recent exponential growth in the value of Bitcoin, many people are investing in this digital currency to hopefully reap huge profits in the future.

In this guide, we will cover the basics of using bitcoin as an investment strategy. Note that we are referring to long-term investment here which is not the same as trading bitcoin for short-term profits.

Investing in the highly volatile cryptocurrency market may not seem like such a good idea for some people. Ideally, you'd have nerves of steel, the discipline and focus to ignore short-term gains, as well as the patience to hold your investment until the right time comes.

If you're really determined to own a small share of the crypto-market, then you should at least know the most suitable methods so you can make the most of your investment.

Bitcoin Investment Methods

Dollar Cost Averaging Method

This strategy is best for beginners to the investing world because you don't need to worry about entering the market at the right time.

You don't have to stress yourself waiting for the price of bitcoin to go down; rather, you just buy at regular time intervals to spread the risk and hold/store your bitcoins in a cold, secure wallet (like a paper wallet or hardware wallet).

For example, if you have an extra $100 to spare every week, you can buy bitcoins every week. Some weeks your $100 may buy you more bitcoin, and some weeks the same amount will buy you less.

This method gives you peace of mind because you don't need to worry about the dips in bitcoin price.

You just have to be disciplined enough to follow your regular schedule and buy when you need to buy without looking at the bitcoin price charts. You don't wait for the price to go down just because you see a downward trend on the charts, you just go right out and buy your bitcoins.

With the dollar cost averaging method, your profits will also average out when you decide to sell your bitcoins. It might not come anywhere close to profits if you invested using the lump sum method, but if you sell at the right time (when the price is high), you'll still make a healthy profit from your investment.

Lump Sum Investing Method

The lump sum method is a much riskier method of investing bitcoins because you will be buying your bitcoins at a single price point.

If you have $100,000 to invest, you will, of course, want to buy the most number of bitcoins, so you wait for the price to go down. *To maximize your investment, you will be compelled to wait for the possible lowest price before buying your bitcoins.*

This method means you will have to 'time' the market, so you buy at just the right time. Of course, this is easier said than done with a volatile commodity like bitcoin. The price varies so much it's extremely difficult to predict when the next price dip is so you can buy at that price.

Trying to time the market can cause a lot of headache and stress to an inexperienced investor. It just brings too many 'what ifs' to mind, such as:

'What if I just wait a few more hours, the price may go down, and I'd be able to buy more bitcoins then.' Or *'What if the price never goes down to the price I want to buy bitcoins at, I'll never be able to buy bitcoins.'*

When it comes to selling off your lump sum investment in the future, you may find it hard to sell as well because you'll be waiting to sell at the right time so you can make the most profit.

You'll try to predict the highest price point, and you'll berate yourself if you sold too soon and lose out on the possibility of much greater profit.

The good thing with lump sum investment method though is if you manage to buy at the lowest possible price and sell at the highest possible price, then you'll make a much bigger profit than if you invested bitcoins using the dollar cost averaging method.

Crypto Hedge Fund Investing Method

If you don't want to trouble yourself with learning the basics of investing using either the dollar cost averaging method or the lump sum method, you might be better off investing your money in a cryptocurrency hedge fund. However, this option is best suited for people who can afford to pay their hefty management and performance fees.

The management fee is paid upfront; some funds require a 2% management fee so if you're investing $100,000, $2,000 of that is going to the management fee which means only $98,000 will be invested in cryptocurrency.

Also, your hedge fund manager will get a percentage of your profits. Some managers require a 20% performance fee so if you profit $50,000 from your investment, $10,000 of that is going to be paid as an incentive fee.

The hedge fund method may not suit everyone, but if you look beyond the fees, you're at least looking at a hands-off approach to investing which could prove to be very profitable for both you and your hedge fund manager.

Strategies To Succeed In Bitcoin Investing

Investing in bitcoin is similar to investing in stocks. Both are high risk and high reward investments which, undoubtedly, is not for everyone.

Bitcoin is even more volatile than stocks so if you want to invest in this cryptocurrency or any other crypto for that matter, you need to know the following strategies to succeed.

Have A Solid Plan In Place

Don't invest blindly and don't invest just because everyone you know has bought bitcoins. When investing, you need to have a good, solid plan in place where you draw your entry point and your exit point.

Your plan will need to be in accordance with the investment method you'll choose to follow. So if you choose the dollar cost averaging method, you need to have a solid plan like how much and how often you'll be buying bitcoins.

For lump sum investing, you need to know in advance at what price you'll be buying your bitcoins and buy at that price (don't wait for it to go any lower). For hedge fund investing, you need to consider the fees you need to pay and know the best time to invest.

Be Prepared For Volatility

This is the number one strategy you need to master. Everyone knows that bitcoin is a highly volatile investment with prices going up and down by hundreds of dollars in mere minutes. You might think to yourself you already know it's going to be volatile because you've seen the charts and the graphs and you've practiced in a demo bitcoin exchange account.

You can handle the risk, you tell yourself. But when you've got thousands of real dollars on the line, it's a very different scenario. Especially if you've worked hard to get those dollars! You might have worked for it for months or years, and there's a very real chance you could lose it all in just a few minutes.

The best thing you can do is to not bother with the dips at all. Just do something that will help you relax and keep your mind off bitcoins because if you don't, you can literally go crazy. Bitcoin investing is like a roller coaster ride; you just need to hold on really, really tight until you get to the end of the ride!

Keep Calm And Don't Panic

Saying this to panicked investors is very easy, but when you're the panicked one, it's a different feeling altogether. The thought of thousands of dollars down the drain is enough to send anyone to a mental breakdown which would, of course, lead to irrational decisions.

If you don't think clearly, you might think of cutting your losses right there and then without thinking of what's going to happen in the long term. If you played your cards right, your bitcoins would be worth so much more than when you paid for it. But you're never going to experience that if you panic and sell early.

Keep Perspective

Investing in bitcoin is a long-term financial activity. It's different from day-to-day trading which involves a lot more technical analysis so a trader can make a nice profit. When investing in bitcoin, you have zoom out of the bitcoin price charts and look at the overall picture. Don't bother looking at the daily, weekly or monthly charts because it's going to bring you nothing but stress.

Look at how far bitcoin rates have come. From literally a few cents when it first started to thousands of dollars now. And experts are saying this upward trend will continue for many more years to come so if you ride out the highs and lows of bitcoin, you'll end up with a very nice investment portfolio in a few years.

Don't Spend What You Can't Lose

This is probably the most important advice you need to take note of. You already know investing in highly volatile cryptocurrencies can either make you insanely rich or bankrupt. But it doesn't have to be these two extremes.

You don't have to invest your entire fortune or your entire life savings in bitcoin or any other cryptocurrency!

> *The most prudent thing you can do is to only invest what you can afford to lose. This means not spending any money that you cannot afford to lose.*

Whether you choose to invest using the dollar cost averaging method, lump sum investing method, or maybe even investing in a crypto hedge fund, don't use money that needs to be used somewhere else.

If you've got money set aside for your retirement, a health fund, an emergency fund, or maybe even your kids' college money, don't even think about touching these funds. So many families have fallen apart because of wrong financial decisions and spent such important funds on risky investments.

If you've done something similar in the past and was able to get away with it, that is, you've made some profits, then don't get cocky and think you can do the same with cryptocurrency. It's a different animal, so to speak. It's the

Wild West of investments right now, and you don't want to lose your hard-earned money.

Patience And Discipline Are Keys To Success

Bitcoin investing is a long-term game. You need to be patient when the bitcoin price goes down, and your investment along with it. If you've looked at bitcoin trends, you'll see it's been in an upward trend since its inception in 2009, so you just need to ride out the troughs until you get to the right crest where you'll be happy to sell your bitcoins.

In the world of Bitcoin investing, there'll be many troughs and crests. You just need the discipline to hold on to your investments and not get scared when prices get too low. Likewise, don't get too excited when the price goes up. A solid plan, patience, and discipline will lead you to bitcoin investing success.

Hindsight Is Always 20/20

Don't berate yourself if you bought at a price much higher than the current bitcoin price. And there's no point getting angry at yourself if you sold your bitcoins too early when the price goes up after you sold.

No one can predict the future. So the best thing for you to do is just aim to make a tidy profit and not think about the 'what ifs' because that's really not going to help you at all.

As they say, hindsight is always 20/20. To put things into perspective, if everyone can see the future, we would all have invested in bitcoins when it was first introduced by Bitcoin founder, Satoshi Nakamoto.

Accepting And Using Bitcoin In Your Business

While many online and brick-and-mortar shops and businesses have added Bitcoin to their payment options, it's still not as widespread as the Bitcoin community would like it to be. Most business owners still prefer traditional payment methods as they simply don't know enough about Bitcoin and what they'd get out of adding it to their business.

Many don't trust Bitcoin and its volatility. They're probably thinking that with such volatile changes in the dollar-bitcoin exchange rates, they would probably end up losing their profits. This fear is understandable, but there have been so many innovations nowadays that this really isn't a concern at all.

After all, many well-known companies like Microsoft, Overstock, Expedia, Wikipedia, Wordpress.com, Shopify, and so much more, are already accepting Bitcoin payments.

Online And Offline Businesses Can Accept Bitcoin Payments

Just because Bitcoin is a virtual currency that is electronic in nature doesn't mean that offline shops can't take advantage of receiving bitcoin payments. For online shops, you can integrate payment processors such as Stripe, Coinbase, Braintree, and more, into your e-commerce site's checkout page.

For offline shops, you can choose from Bitcoin terminals or Point-Of-Sale apps such as XBTerminal, Coinify or Coingate. You can also print out QR codes that your customers can scan with their mobile wallets and easily pay you in bitcoins.

Once your bitcoin wallet is set up, all you have to do is announce to the whole world you're ready to accept Bitcoin payments!

How To Handle The Volatility Of Bitcoin

The thought of losing your profits and essentially giving away your merchandise for free to your customers is one scary thought as you can quickly go bankrupt if all your customers paid in bitcoin.

At one point in time it may have been true, but with Bitcoin payment processors like Coinbase and BitPay, it's now possible to receive your payments in bitcoin and have it instantly converted to US dollars or any other supported currency. This way you avoid all the risks associated with bitcoin and receive the full dollar amount you're supposed to receive.

To illustrate, if your customer pays you $100 worth of bitcoin for a pair of jeans, then you're going to receive exactly $100 in your bank account. The payment gateway you use, for example BitPay, will shield you from bitcoin's volatility so you always get the full dollar amount.

For the more enterprising business owners who can handle Bitcoin's unpredictability, the opportunity to make even more profit from the bitcoins they've been paid with might be irresistible.

If you belong to this category, you would probably choose to keep your bitcoins in your digital wallets, and forego the use of a payment processor who will automatically convert your bitcoins to dollars.

Why Your Business Should Start Accepting Bitcoin Payments

Bitcoin was created by Satoshi Nakamoto in response to the 2008 financial market crash which almost crippled the entire global economy. He created it to solve or overcome the problems we have with having a centralized banking system that benefited banks more than they did consumers.

Just think about the bank fees you have to pay everytime someone pays you for your product or service. Deposit fees, withdrawal fees, transaction fees, credit card fees, and all sorts of fees are deducted from your hard-earned money.

Bitcoin's purpose was to avoid all that, and this peer-to-peer electronic cash system was Satoshi Nakamoto's solution to the problem. The system was created essentially so that everyone gets what is due them without the unnecessary intervention of banks and government.

The Benefits Of Bitcoin Payments For Your Business

There are plenty of benefits for your business if you choose to start accepting bitcoin payments. Here are some of them:

No Risk Of Chargebacks

Paypal, credit and debit card payments leave your business vulnerable to chargebacks. Most, if not all, businesses (both online and offline merchants) have probably experienced this problem at one point or another. Dealing with a chargeback is a headache-inducing and time-consuming process.

Your customers can claim to not recognize the charge on their card statements, or their card was stolen and somebody else used it to buy from you, or they're upset that your merchandise was not as described or it was defective.

Some people simply like to do chargebacks because they want to get an item for free, especially if it's a high-value item. Of course, this is a very unethical thing to do, but you can't predict your customers' behaviors.

With Bitcoin payments, there is zero risk of chargebacks because all payments, once it has been confirmed, are final. There is no way for anyone, not even the savviest and smartest programmers in the world, can reverse or undo a bitcoin transaction.

Bitcoin payments offer merchant protection that is unparalleled by any other payment option available today. No bank and no government can give you the level of merchant protection that Bitcoin does.

No Fraud And Double Payments

The Bitcoin network is an extremely secure payment system. Unlike banks, Bitcoin is incorruptible. Before Bitcoin came along, double payments and fraud were a very real problem with digital cash but luckily, thanks to the efforts of Satoshi Nakamoto, the problem of double spending was finally solved.

Bitcoin is a decentralized, peer-to-peer payment system. Everyone on the network sees all the bitcoin transactions that have ever taken place. This transparency makes it difficult for fraudsters to fake records so they can spend the same amount of bitcoins twice or double spend it.

This massive ledger, also known as the blockchain, keeps a record of all transactions. A transaction is only added to a block once it has been confirmed or verified by miners that the transaction is valid.

Near Instant Payments

Bitcoin payments are fast, irrevocable and final. There's no way for anyone to undo any bitcoin transaction. As long you indicate the correct bitcoin address for your customers to pay into, you're good to go, and your bitcoins will arrive in your wallet usually within 10-45 minutes.

Using the correct bitcoin address is obviously a very important point to consider because if by any chance, you present the wrong bitcoin address, then there's no way for you to recover those bitcoins. Unless of course, you know who owns that bitcoin address, then you can simply ask them to send those bitcoins to your correct address.

Another upside to using payment gateways like Coinbase and BitPay is that you can receive your cash in your bank accounts within 2-3 days. These services usually send payments every business day (not everytime a transaction occurs).

Alternatively, if you want to keep your bitcoins, that is, you don't want to convert them to dollars, then that's perfectly fine. You can select this option in your payment gateway settings. Either way, you're going to get your bitcoins or your dollars very conveniently and in less time than if the customer paid with Paypal or a credit card.

Negligible Transaction Fees

With bitcoin payments, you get to keep more of what your customer pays you. You effectively cut out the middleman (your bank) with their expensive fees. You will still need to pay a very small bitcoin transaction fee which goes to the miners who verify all bitcoin transactions and add it to the ledger or blockchain.

> *This transaction fee is almost negligible and is a mere equivalent to cents, unlike the fees your bank or credit card company requires you to pay!*

For credit card payments, merchants are usually charged an interchange fee (paid to the bank or card issuer) and an assessment fee (paid to the credit card company such as Visa or Mastercard). On average, these fees will end up costing the merchant around 3% to 4% per transaction.

In comparison, for bitcoin transactions, the fees are typically around 10,000 Satoshis or 0.0001 bitcoin. You're free to set your own fees, but the higher the transaction fee you set per transaction, the faster bitcoin miners will confirm your transaction.

For a $1,000 credit card payment, the fees that merchants have to pay would be around $30 to $40. For a similar purchase amount paid for in bitcoin, the transaction fee would roughly be around $1 if the current bitcoin price is say, for example, $10,000 per bitcoin ($10,000 x 0.0001 = $1).

You can already see just by this example that bitcoin transactions will save you a lot of money just in transaction fees. Imagine how much you will get to save if you're able to sell your $1,000 product just 10 times a day or 100 times a day!

Increased Sales And More Profit For You

Bitcoin doesn't discriminate where anyone comes from. Even if your customer lives in a country known for credit card fraud, in Bitcoin's eyes everyone is equal. If you've ever tried to accept payments from customers in these countries, you know just how difficult and cumbersome the entire process is.

Paypal, Stripe and other popular payment gateways don't accept or support many countries with high prevalence of fraud. But with Bitcoin, you can easily accept payments from anyone who lives anywhere in the world. All they need to pay you is just your bitcoin address!

They don't need to send their photos and national ID cards, so your customers' privacy is well protected. And as you already know, all bitcoin transactions are final, so there's no way for any of your customers to do a chargeback like they easily can with a credit card.

Bitcoin makes the world a smaller and better place. It erases borders, government red tape, and bureaucracy. It allows merchants and business owners like you to receive payments from customers who are unfortunate enough to live in countries with a high fraud rate.

Bitcoin protects you and your business. At the same time, it allows you to provide your service and your products to everyone in the whole world.

Happier Customers

Adding Bitcoin to your list of supported payments will give your customers an extra choice to hand over their money to you. Even if they don't have bitcoins yet, they might eventually get into the game sooner or later.

And when they do, they'll remember you and recommend you to their friends. Even existing customers will be happy to know you've added Bitcoin payments.

If you're one of the few businesses in your community that accepts Bitcoin payments, then you're probably going to become popular because you'll be viewed as an innovative and forward-thinking business.

Many people have heard about Bitcoin on the news, and many would have developed a passing interest or have begun to become curious about bitcoins and cryptocurrency in general. You can educate your customers and let them know what Bitcoin is and how it will help them in their financial transactions.

Think about it, would you rather be one of the first businesses to offer Bitcoin payments and steal your competitor's customers in the process? Or would you rather have your customers go to your competition simply because they offer Bitcoin payments, and you don't?

Get Support From The Bitcoin Community

The Bitcoin community is growing fast, and with skyrocketing bitcoin prices, they are looking for places where they can spend their bitcoins. A number of big companies have added Bitcoin to their payment options, but a great majority of businesses have yet to follow suit. So when the Bitcoin community discovers a new business that supports bitcoin, they share the news with everyone. That's free advertisement for your business, and you can expect them to drop by your website or physical store anytime soon.

To get sufficient exposure to the Bitcoin community, you can spread the news on social media, in Bitcoin forums, pages, groups, etc. If you have a physical store, you should also put a large signboard outside that will announce to anyone passing by that you're accepting Bitcoin payments.

Growing your business doesn't have to be difficult. Accepting Bitcoin payments will not only make your business popular among the Bitcoin community, but it will also lead to more sales and more profits for you.

How To Protect Yourself Against Fraud And Theft

Bitcoin and cryptocurrencies are hot commodities right now. Everyone wants a piece of the action, though with soaring prices, many can't afford to buy and invest out of their own pockets.

So they do the next best thing they can think of – scam and steal these precious digital coins from other people. In this guide, we'll show you some of the most common scams these con artists are running as well as how you can protect yourself against them.

Bitcoin And Cryptocurrencies Are Not Scams

Before we go into the main scams you should be aware of, we'd like to point out that these scams are all from outside forces, and not cryptocurrencies themselves. You might hear some people say that cryptocurrencies are nothing but a huge scam but it's 100% false, and we'll explain why.

The technology behind cryptocurrencies is called the blockchain. It is an incorruptible digital ledger that records all transactions in the network. No central body controls it. It is transparent, and anyone can track any transaction that has ever happened in the past.

No one can alter any transaction recorded on the blockchain because doing so would mean you'd have to alter the rest of the transactions or blocks that came after that particular transaction; this is virtually an impossible task to do.

The blockchain is so secure that many banks and startup companies are now experimenting, and starting to implement blockchain technology because they've seen just how well it works on Bitcoin and cryptocurrencies.

Now that you know you can trust the technology behind cryptocurrencies, let's discuss the most common scams that many people fall prey to.

Scam #1 – Fake Bitcoin Exchanges

There are plenty of reputable bitcoin exchanges today. The biggest and most popular platforms that have been around a few years are Coinbase, Kraken, CEX.io, Changelly, Bitstamp, Poloniex, and Bitfinex. With that being said, we cannot vouch for any company even if they're well known in the industry.

You will have to do your due diligence by researching the company's history, user reviews, and determine for yourself whether you want to spend your hard-earned fiat money with them.

Too Good To Be True Exchange Rates

Due to the highly volatile nature of cryptocurrencies (prices can go up and down by a huge spread in just a few hours!), many unsavory characters on the Internet are capitalizing on this volatility. They prey on unsuspecting beginners who can't spot the difference between a legitimate exchange and a fake one.

These fake bitcoin exchanges can easily put up nice-looking websites and impress people with their seemingly sophisticated look. They hook people in with their promises of lower-than-market-rate prices and guaranteed returns. Simply put, they play on people's greed.

Imagine how ecstatic you'd feel if you found out about a website that offers bitcoins at 10% or 20% lower rates than the going rates on Coinbase or Kraken. If these large platforms are offering $15,000 for 1 bitcoin, and this other site is offering it at $12,000, wouldn't you jump at the chance?

You'd save so much ($3,000 per bitcoin!), and you can use your savings to buy even more bitcoins. See, that's them playing on greed! They know that people want to buy more bitcoins for less dollars. And who can blame those poor victims? If we didn't know any better, we might fall for the same scam too.

Receive Instant PayPal Payment For Your Bitcoins

Another method these fake bitcoin exchanges use to steal your bitcoins is they'll offer to buy your coins at higher-than-market-rates, and then send the equivalent dollar amount to your PayPal address.

To the unsuspecting bitcoin owner, he thinks he's getting the better end of the deal because he's going to get more money for his bitcoins, and he'll get the cash instantly in his PayPal account.

So, he enters the amount of bitcoins he wants to sell, confirms he's happy with the equivalent dollar amount, types in his PayPal address so they can send the money to him, then he waits. And waits. And waits some more.

He'll contact the website but, of course, they're not going to reply to him now because they have his bitcoins (remember, all bitcoin transactions are final and irreversible once validated).

At this point, he'll realize he's just been scammed. He can report the site and write bad reviews, but who's he kidding? These savvy scammers will just set up shop under a new domain name and wait for their next victim.

> *The key takeaway here is to stay away from 'exchanges' with too-good-to-be-true rates. As the saying goes, if it's too good to be true, it probably is.*

Scam #2 – Phishing Scams

There are so many kinds of phishing scams that run rampant today. Ever received an email from your 'bank' asking you verify or update your account details to make sure your details remain up to date? And that you have to click on the email link to update your details?

Many people are aware these types of emails are nothing more than a scam. Modern email services send these junk emails to the junk folder anyway, so you don't see them all that much nowadays.

But with Bitcoin and cryptocurrency being so new and so hot in the news right now, scammers are scrambling to find a way to steal your bitcoins by getting access to your digital wallets!

Email Phishing Scams

Scammers will send you an email designed to make it look like it came from your online wallet service (this is why we don't suggest storing large sums of virtual currency in your exchange wallets).

In the email, they'll ask you to click on a link which will lead you to a fake website. It will look exactly like your exchange or wallet website. Of course, it's not the same because the domain name will be different.

For example, if you're using Coinbase, they'll use a similar misspelled domain such as:

- Cooinbase
- Coiinbase
- Coinbasse
- Coinsbase
- Coinbase-Client-Update.com
- or something similar…

It will also most probably not have a security feature called SSL installed, which means the domain will start with HTTP and not HTTPS (modern browsers like Chrome and Firefox should warn you if it's a secure site or not).

If you fall for this phishing scam, and you log in to the fake wallet site, then the scammers now have your login details to your real wallet! They can easily lock you out of your account, and they'll then have the freedom to transfer every single bitcoin you own to their own wallets.

Malware Scams

In this type of scam, scammers will ask you to click on a link either via email, banner ad, forum ad, or anywhere they can post a link which will then download a type of malware to your computer.

Often, these malwares are keyloggers which will record everything you type on your computer, and send the information to the scammers. So, if you log in to your online wallet, like Coinbase for example, they will be able to see your username and your password, and they can then log in to your account and easily steal your coins from you!

> *The key takeaway for protecting yourself from these types of scams is to never click on links from untrustworthy sources.*

If you don't recognize the sender, or the website domain name is misspelled, it should raise a red flag, and you should report the email and/or leave the phishing site right away.

Furthermore, consider using offline storing methods such as paper wallets or hardware wallets so even if scammers get access to your online wallet, they'll have nothing to steal there.

Scam #3 – Cloud Mining Scams

Cloud mining is a popular way of becoming a bitcoin miner. You no longer need to invest in your own supercomputer and join a mining group to solve complex cryptographic hash problems. You don't even need to worry about expensive electricity bills.

You simply need to sign up to a cloud mining service (also known as a mining farm), rent mining equipment, and receive payments proportionate to your subscription.

While some cloud mining companies are legitimate, there are many fly-by-night websites which promise unrealistic returns for measly sums, whose sole purpose is to steal your money.

Some common red flags to watch out for when looking to join a cloud mining service is the absence of an About page, Terms of Use/Service page, physical address, and/or contact number.

They might also not have a secure domain (no HTTPS before their domain name). These details are all very important in figuring out which site is a scam and which is not. You can search Google for reviews and go through their website to get a feel if they're legitimate or not. More often than not, these sites would be anonymous with no names or faces behind them.

Some may appear legitimate at first but take a deeper look at what your investment's going to get you. You may pay eventually sign up for a contract which is going to cost you a few thousand dollars a year but what are you going to get in return? You'll have to do the math yourself and calculate if you're going to end up in the green.

The key takeaway here is before you spend any of your hard-earned fiat money, you should at least make sure you're dealing with a legitimate company and not some anonymous scammer who'll leave you in tears.

Do plenty of research, read reviews, and browse the crypto-mining communities for information on the best and most trustworthy cloud mining companies.

Scam #4 – Ponzi Scams

Ponzi scams are probably easier to spot than the other scams we've covered so far in this guide. This is because Ponzi scams are well known for guaranteeing outlandish returns on investments with little to no risk to the investors. People fall for these sorts of scams all the time because people want guaranteed returns on their investments.

With Bitcoin and cryptocurrency, any company that guarantees exponential returns on any investment should be viewed as a potential scammer. The cryptocurrency market is highly volatile, and one minute the price could be at an all-time high and the next, it's down by a few hundred or a few thousand dollars.

Because of this volatility, you should never believe anyone who tells you you're guaranteed a 10% return on your investment every single day, or whatever the scammer's terms may be.

Since Ponzi schemes rely on new members, a.k.a. victims, to pay off their early investors, they usually offer incentives for members to recruit new people to join their network.

It's very common for scams like this to offer some form of affiliate rewards. You refer someone to invest in the 'company,' and you get compensated for your efforts.

Some Ponzi schemes guarantee daily profits *forever*. If this seems impossible, it most certainly is. No one even knows if bitcoins will be around that long and guaranteeing daily returns is just crazy. Right off the bat, an intelligent investor will see that offers like these are nothing more than scams designed to rip you off your money or your bitcoins.

In fact, many of these scam sites prefer bitcoin payments because they know Bitcoin transactions can't be reversed or canceled once sent! Either way, whether they require fiat or cryptocurrency, know who you're sending your money to first.

The key takeaway here is if you know the company's offers are too good to be true, then you should run away in the opposite direction. Sometimes, there's just no point in even looking up reviews on the Internet when it comes to scams like these because most 'reviewers' are those who got in the game early and thus have already received some return on their investment.

And usually, when these users leave reviews they'll include their affiliate link so you know right away they have a vested interest for leaving glowing reviews for a company they may, or may not know, is a scam.

The Future Of Cryptocurrency

Before we talk about the future of cryptocurrency, it's important to remind ourselves of the past and what cryptocurrency was like in the beginning. Back in 2008, when Bitcoin founder, Satoshi Nakamoto, first released his whitepaper on Bitcoin, many people said it was just a fad and a scam designed to trick people into giving up their 'real' money.

There were many naysayers and financial experts who said Bitcoin will never be adopted by the masses and will fizzle and die out in a year or so.

Fortunately, the cryptocurrency community rallied and worked together to make Bitcoin a success. They saw potential in the blockchain technology and what it could mean for the finance sector. They saw the need for cryptocurrency because the current financial setup via banks and governments had too many problems and was causing national economies to collapse.

They saw that keeping inflation at bay was difficult with traditional currencies and the poorest people often have no easy access to banks. Receiving or sending payments was oftentimes a headache with transaction fees eating up a significant amount of money.

Banks charge exorbitant fees just so their customers can get access to their very own money, and the government takes very little action, if at all, to help the people.

Bitcoin supporters say the modern financial system is a mess where banks and governments collude or work together, not to help their citizens' financial needs, but to take as much money as they can from them in terms of fees collected.

Bitcoin changed all that. With Bitcoin, you're cutting out the middleman. There are no more banks to deal with and no government to spy on your bank accounts. With Bitcoin, you are your own bank. You're the bank teller sending and receiving payments, and you're the banker in charge of keeping your money safe.

Bitcoin has been a leader on so many fronts. As the first successful cryptocurrency, it has paved the way for other cryptocurrencies to succeed and the global community has slowly taken notice these past few years. Read on to find out what other possibilities Bitcoin and cryptocurrencies bring for the future!

Massive Support From The Masses

In most developed countries, getting a credit card or a business loan is relatively easy. However, in developing countries, you'd have to literally jump through hoops and government red tape before you can get one. But with Bitcoin and cryptocurrency, all you need is just your digital wallet, and you can start receiving cryptocurrency from anyone, anywhere in the world.

You don't even need your own Internet connection at home; you can simply go somewhere with good Internet access and create a quick wallet online or on your mobile phone. Of course, storing your crypto online is not a good idea so you should look into storing these in cold storage, such as a hardware wallet or paper wallet.

But online wallets are great for small transactions so if you need to pay a utility bill or your credit card bill, simply scan the utility company's bitcoin wallet's QR code and send your crypto payment. No need to spend the whole day standing in long lines!

Today, there are already many businesses which have started to accept bitcoin payments (though they are still in the minority). These forward-thinking business owners see the benefit of accepting bitcoins and are profiting nicely from this smart business decision!

You can buy virtually anything with bitcoins. You can buy plane tickets, you can rent cars, you can pay for your college tuition, you can buy groceries, you can buy stuff on Amazon by purchasing Amazon gift cards on third-party sites, and so much more!

> *In the future, we can expect so many more businesses to jump onto the bitcoin payment wagon, and it would be a win-win situation for both business owners and customers.*

Businesses will get their payment fast and into their bank accounts the very next day (using a payment gateway like BitPay which offers instant bitcoins to fiat currency conversion), and customers will get to buy items in a very convenient manner.

Bitcoin In Developing Economies

It's not surprising that Bitcoin has seen massive adoption in recent years. In fact, in Zimbabwe, people are using bitcoins to make financial transactions. With the demise of the Zimbabwean dollar, the country had to resort to using US dollars as their main currency.

However, this is not a very feasible solution because their government can't print US dollars themselves. Venezuelans are also experiencing the same problem. The Venezuelan bolivar has become so hyper-inflated it's almost unusable. People have resorted to using bitcoins to pay for basic goods, medicines, groceries, and so much more.

For the Zimbabweans and Venezuelans, as well as the Vietnamese, Colombians, and citizens of countries with super inflated currencies, Bitcoin is a beacon of light because it's not subject to the whims and manipulations of their local banks or their governments.

Their present economic situation is a perfect example of the downside of having a central authority to manage a country's currency, while at the same time, it highlights all the benefits of using Bitcoin, a decentralized and 100% transparent financial network.

With Bitcoin getting massive support from people in developing countries, governments may soon be stepping in to regulate the use of Bitcoin and other cryptocurrencies. While we can't predict the future, for now, Bitcoin provides a wonderful inflation-less alternative to traditional currency.

> *And with skyrocketing Bitcoin and cryptocurrency prices, this gives many people a lot of purchasing power which their national currencies can't provide.*

Fast And Cheap International Payments

One of the main benefits of bitcoin payments is the speed by which the recipient can get their bitcoins. This is perfect for people who hire freelancers or employees overseas.

The employees don't need to sign up for a bank account and incur fees left and right just because they're receiving money from yourself, an international client.

Of course, we must not fail to mention the fees that you yourself will be paying to your bank everytime you remit or transfer monies to your overseas workers.

In addition to the fees both you and your recipient pay, you'd also have to factor in the exchange rate. Most banks and money transfer services will usually tell you up front that "this" is the current exchange rate but when you compare it to actual rates, the bank rate would be much lower.

Even for PayPal payments, you'll notice a difference in the exchange rate they use. You probably won't notice the exchange rate when you're transferring relatively small amounts, but when you're transacting in thousands of dollars, the fees can very quickly add up to a significant amount.

With Bitcoin, you can say goodbye to all these exorbitant fees.

For every bitcoin transaction, you do need to pay a small fee for the miners, but it's literally nothing compared to what your banks are charging you! Whether you're sending 1,000 bitcoins or 0.01 bitcoins, the mining fee can be the same since the fee is computed in terms of bytes, not the amount of bitcoins.

The size (in bytes) of your transaction will depend on the number of inputs and outputs per transaction. Without going into the technical details, what's important to take note here is the mining fees are very, very small compared to your bank's fees. This is why Bitcoin and cryptocurrency are going to change the future. More people will transact with each other directly to avoid paying those very expensive bank fees!

With more and more people sending cryptocurrency to each other directly, there may be no more need for third-party money transfer services or even banks. Though this may take many years to happen, it's still a possibility once everyone gets educated on the benefits of using cryptocurrency to send and receive payments from anyone in the world in just a few minutes.

Combat Crime and Corruption

Many people are worried that the Bitcoin network is being used by money launderers, criminals, and corrupt officials because they think it's an anonymous network. Yes, all verified transactions are recorded on the blockchain and no, there are no names listed there.

You can see only alphanumeric codes, lots of it in fact. If you download the free and open source Bitcoin Core client, you'll also need to download the entire blockchain which is already more than 100GB+. Millions of bitcoin transactions since 2009 are stored on the blockchain. You'll even see the first ever transaction by its founder, Satoshi Nakamoto.

We're mentioning this to point to the fact that Bitcoin is not really anonymous. Instead, it's pseudonymous, meaning users can hide behind pseudonyms, but on close inspection, digital forensics experts can trace who owns Bitcoin wallets.

This is, of course, a time-consuming endeavor but when you're after criminals who've laundered millions or billions of dollars' worth of bitcoins then catching them becomes a top priority. In fact, experts say that criminals are better off stashing their stolen loot in offshore bank accounts with their super strict bank privacy laws.

But bitcoin is easier to move around so people think they can easily hide their illicit transactions in the alphanumeric maze known as the blockchain. In short, a number of criminals have been put behind bars thanks to Bitcoin and the blockchain.

In the future, if and when cryptocurrency gains massive support and adoption from the masses worldwide, it will be easier for authorities to trace and catch criminals hoping to use cryptocurrencies as a means to hide and move their stolen money around.

Blockchain Technology Will Become Mainstream

Many governments, banks, and private organizations are looking into adopting the blockchain technology into their products and services. The blockchain is the underlying technology behind Bitcoin and other cryptocurrencies.

> *The technology is already starting to receive recognition and adoption from many sectors in the world. While this may take several years, it's at least a positive nod in favor of the blockchain revolution.*

Two of the most popular blockchain technologies today are Ethereum and Hyperledger. You may have heard of Ethereum as the second most popular cryptocurrency, after Bitcoin. But it's more than just a virtual currency platform.

Ethereum is a platform that allows anyone to create smart contracts which help people trade or exchange anything of value, such as money, property, stocks, etc. The contract is publicly transparent and is recorded on the blockchain which means other people are witness to the agreement.

The best thing about smart contracts is you are basically automating contracts without paying for the services of a middleman such as a bank, stockbroker, or lawyer.

Hyperledger, on the other hand, is an open source, cross-industry collaborative project with contributors from many major companies such as Deutsche Bank, IBM, Airbus and SAP.

According to their website, the collaboration aims to develop a "new generation of transactional applications that establish trust, accountability and transparency." These applications have the potential to streamline business processes and reduce the cost and complexity of various systems in the real world.

These are just a few examples of how blockchain technology is going to change the world in the future. Blockchain may be less than a decade old, but it has already changed the lives of so many people for the better.

Will You Be A Part Of Cryptocurrency Revolution?

In this guide, you've learned so many benefits of using Bitcoin, cryptocurrency and blockchain technology. Investing in cryptocurrency may be in your best interest though it's always best to do in-depth research on which cryptocurrency to invest in.

Bitcoin may be too expensive for now but remember that you don't have to buy a whole bitcoin. Alternatively, there are other emerging cryptocurrencies with good track records you may consider investing in.

With cryptocurrency looking set to get integrated with mainstream financial markets, investing in cryptocurrency is not a scary thought anymore. In fact, it just might be the best financial decision you'll ever make for yourself and your family's future.